International
TERRORISTS

International
TERRORISTS

Thomas Streissguth

illustrated with photographs

The Oliver Press, Inc.,
Minneapolis

The Oliver Press
Josiah King House
2709 Lyndale Avenue South
Minneapolis, MN 55408

Library of Congress Cataloging-in-Publication Data

Streissguth, Thomas, 1958-
International terrorists / Thomas Streissguth.
p. cm. — (Profiles)
Includes bibliographical references and index.
  Summary: Examines the lives of various contemporary
terrorist leaders and the violent tactics of such groups as the Irish
Republican Army, the Baader Meinhof gang, and the Hezbollah.
ISBN 1-881508-07-2 : $14.95
1. Terrorism—Juvenile literature. 2. Terrorists—Juvenile
literature. [1. Terrorism. 2. Terrorists.] I. Title.
II. Series: Profiles (Minneapolis, Minn.)
HV6431.S77   1993   92-45139
909.82—dc20   CIP
                                                                          AC

ISBN 1-881508-07-2
Profiles V
Printed in the United States of America

99 98 97 96 95 94 93   8 7 6 5 4 3 2 1

Contents

Because they are symbols of authority, national leaders such as France's King Louis XVI have long been terrorist targets.

Introduction

*P*olitical violence is an old tradition in human history. The ancient Greeks believed that the murder of a tyrant was a noble act. Rulers during the Middle Ages used poison and the knife to dispose of their enemies. Military commanders have ordered the mass execution of civilians to stop rebellions and to win over foreign populations. Fear, one of the most powerful human emotions, is also a useful weapon.

Modern terrorism began during the French Revolution. In 1793, after the execution of King Louis XVI, France's revolutionary government set up a Committee of Public Safety to deal with their enemies. The committee was led by a fanatic named Maximilien Robespierre. Through the Committee of Public Safety, Robespierre set a grim example for those who would oppose the new French republic.

Maximilien Robespierre's uncompromising righteousness and willingness to use extreme violence for political goals set an example for later terrorists. Ironically, in his lifetime Robespierre was known as "The Incorruptible."

The committee ordered the arrest of thousands of nobles, commoners, foreigners, and supporters of the royalty. People from all walks of life were thrown into prison. Then the committee condemned to death those found guilty of threatening the revolution—either through their words, their actions, or their station in life. After a short trial, revolutionary guards drove the prisoners in carts through the streets of Paris, the French capital, to a crowded public square.

In the middle of the square stood a *guillotine*, a tall device with a wooden frame, a bench, ropes and pulleys, and a heavy, sharp blade. The prisoner was forced to lay down on the bench and was pushed underneath the blade. Revolutionary guards stood at attention as an official read the sentence to the gathered spectators. An executioner then carried out the sentence by releasing the heavy blade. The prisoner was instantly beheaded. For months, the executions continued. The French called this time *le Terreur:* the "Reign of Terror."

The committee used the Reign of Terror to strike fear into their enemies and to keep their hold on the revolutionary government. Although Robespierre himself died on the guillotine, and his Committee of Public Safety eventually lost power, the people of Europe never forgot the Reign of Terror.

In the late nineteenth century, terrorists attacked British officials during the fight for Irish independence. In 1881, Russian assassins murdered their own ruler, Tsar Alexander II, in an attempt to overthrow the Russian government. Although the Russian assassins failed in this mission, the Russian people did succeed in overthrowing the tsarist government in 1917. The communists who took power then built their own regime through the use of mass executions and prison camps.

After the end of World War II in 1945, many people believed that diplomacy and negotiation would finally end the use of violence and war. But an explosion of terrorism occurred during the 1970s and 1980s. With television offering a means of rapid, worldwide communication in images and words, terrorists had the opportunity to spread fear all over the world. The hijacking,

Although the precise number is unknown, estimates say that during the French Reign of Terror (1793-1794) more than 15,000 people met their deaths on the guillotine.

bombing, and kidnapping of innocent people proved a useful way of fighting for a cause—whether it was nationhood for the Palestinians of the Middle East, the unification of southern and northern Ireland, or the establishment of a communist regime in Peru.

10

Terrorists frightened the world's wealthy and peaceful nations. It seemed that no place and no person could be completely safe from these random acts of violence. Countries that had promised never to deal with terrorists came under intense pressure to meet demands and negotiate for hostages. The terrorists were winning—with the weapon of worldwide publicity.

Perhaps the use of terror will decline in the 1990s and beyond. Computers now link police forces and provide valuable information. Stricter security at airports and other public places gives terrorists fewer opportunities to carry out their plans. Yet terrorist incidents still take place, and many violent terrorist organizations are still intact. New conflicts are erupting in the Middle East and in eastern Europe, providing combatants with new grievances and new targets for terrorist attacks. As long as political conflict exists, some people will choose violence to attain their goals.

In 1872, Sergei Nechaev poses for a rare photograph shortly before his arrest in Switzerland.

1

Sergei Nechaev

*F*or 50 years after the French Revolution, European rulers lived in the shadow of Robespierre's terror. The guillotine symbolized the dangers of a popular revolution. Kingdoms and empires took harsh measures against those who demanded an end to monarchy. Nevertheless, in 1848, violent revolts broke out in Germany, Austria, and France. Many Europeans sought new constitutions that would establish elected, representative governments. In some European nations, they succeeded.

In the Russian Empire, however, conditions were different. The Russian tsar ruled without a constitution, a parliament, or elections. Censorship and prison were the tsar's answers to dissent and protest.

In 1847, a year before republican revolts swept

across Europe, Sergei Nechaev was born in the Russian town of Ivanovo. Lying 200 miles northeast of Moscow, this city was a center of Russia's textile industry. Nechaev's own grandparents were former serfs, or farm laborers, who had bought their freedom from their owners.

Nechaev, whose father was a sign painter and a part-time waiter, detested Ivanovo's noisy factories and dreary neighborhoods. While still a young man, he joined a circle of teachers and intellectuals. The members of the group often spoke about the need for revolutionary changes in Russia.

Nechaev's energy and stubbornness impressed his friends in Ivanovo. He became famous for his strength of will and for his dedication to a Russian revolution. Many years of poverty and hard work had also given him a streak of vengefulness.

In 1861, Nechaev and several of the city's teachers began a school for factory workers. Many such schools, in which teachers instructed factory workers in reading and writing, were opening around the Russian Empire. However, the schools raised the suspicions of the tsar and the Russian government. Educated workers could easily become dissatisfied—even dangerous. In June 1862, after only a few months, the tsar ordered all of the factory schools to be closed down. Several of Nechaev's friends left Ivanovo for Moscow.

Although he worked at several menial jobs, Nechaev was unable to support himself. Since his father earned little, Sergei became a costly expense for his family. Humiliated by the family for not earning his keep, Nechaev felt a growing resentment toward society in general.

After acquiring the passport necessary for travel within Russia, Nechaev moved to Moscow in the summer of 1865. There he found cheap lodgings and began studying for a teaching certificate. But after failing the teaching examination, he moved to the capital of St. Petersburg.

There Nechaev discovered that the city's students had organized an entire revolutionary underground. Members of this underground divided themselves into small groups, or cells, and followed the instructions of a single leader. They accepted the need for violence to achieve a more just Russian society. Some among them proposed a simple solution to Russia's troubles—they would kill the Russian tsar.

Nikolai Ishutin, the leader of one of these revolutionary cells, ordered his followers to commit acts of violence against soldiers, policemen, ministers, and other officials. If the government responded with harsh measures, Ishutin believed, a popular revolution would quickly be touched off.

On April 4, 1866, Dmitri Karakozov—one of Ishutin's followers—attempted to assassinate the tsar. Karakozov failed, but his act inspired Sergei Nechaev to join the underground in St. Petersburg. The poor student from Ivanovo quickly formed a small, loyal circle around him. Although he had finally won his teaching certificate, Nechaev no longer planned to make teaching his career.

Nechaev led meetings and wrote revolutionary pamphlets. He controlled his circle with threats and intrigue—the methods of a dictator. With the help of other Russian revolutionaries, he planned a popular uprising for February 1870—the 200th anniversary of a famous Russian peasant revolt.

Nechaev quickly became known to the Third Section—the tsar's secret police. In January 1869, they arrested and questioned him. Although he was released, Nechaev saw his arrest as an opportunity to spread his fame as a revolutionary.

After leaving police custody, Nechaev wrote a note claiming that the authorities had arrested him and had exiled him to distant Siberia. He then dropped the note from a carriage that was carrying him along a busy St. Petersburg street. A passerby found the note and brought it to the members of Nechaev's circle. The note transformed Nechaev from a little-known student leader into a famous "political prisoner."

In fact, Nechaev managed to slip across the Russian border with a false passport in March 1869. Soon after his escape from Russia, the Third Section arrested many of his followers. This brought the operations of his group to a complete halt.

Nechaev traveled to Geneva, Switzerland, where a circle of Russian revolutionaries—including the famous

Mikhail Alexandrovich Bakunin inspired much of the terroristic activity in nineteenth-century Russia, including that of Nechaev.

anarchist Mikhail Bakunin—were living in exile. Soon after Nechaev arrived, he visited Bakunin. Nechaev's commitment to the Russian revolution convinced Bakunin to take the younger man under his protection.

Bakunin and Nechaev agreed that murder and arson, carried out by dedicated revolutionaries, could spark a revolution in Russia. This underground terrorism would, they believed, bring about a crackdown by the police and the army. In the panic that followed, Russian workers and peasants would topple the Russian government.

17

Bakunin and Nechaev wrote proclamations exhorting the Russian people to resist their government. They sent the proclamations to Germany, where their associates mailed them to hundreds of people inside Russia.

Nechaev's real goal was to use Bakunin and the other Russian exiles for his own purposes. To impress Bakunin, Nechaev described himself as the leader of a vast underground network. He claimed that his movement was planning to destroy Russia's existing institutions and to murder military leaders, business leaders, and police agents.

In cooperation with Bakunin, Nechaev wrote a small pamphlet that served as a guide for those working underground to overthrow the tsar. They called this book *Catechism of a Revolutionary*. In this work, Nechaev described in detail the life of a dedicated revolutionary: He or she would renounce all friendships and property and live solely for the pleasure of destruction.

Within the book, Nechaev also invented an organizational system for his underground. A primary "cell" would be made up of five or six members. Each member would begin another cell, but the members of these cells could communicate only with their leader—never with members of another cell. In this way, terrorists would never know about the plans of the other groups. This would prevent cell members, should they be captured by the police, from revealing information about the organization.

Nechaev wrote *Catechism of a Revolutionary* in code and had it smuggled into Russia. It remained a favorite work of revolutionary terrorists well into the twentieth century.

In the summer of 1869, Nechaev slipped back into Russia and made his way to Moscow. Now a famous revolutionary, he easily convinced students and workers to join him. He approached many wealthy students— whom he could blackmail if necessary. After stealing their letters, Nechaev could keep his followers in line by threatening to expose their actions to the police.

In Moscow, Nechaev founded the Society of the People's Revenge. He set up committees to handle finances, recruiting, strategy, and other important matters. He also announced to his followers that an executive committee had been formed, and that the decisions of this committee on all matters were final. Unknown to the others, however, Nechaev was the only member of the executive committee. He alone made all the important decisions.

Nechaev's methods turned many of his followers against him. One of these—a student named Ivanov— had opposed posting copies of Nechaev's revolutionary proclamations in Moscow. Ivanov believed that this would lead to trouble with the police. Eventually, Ivanov threatened to leave the group and to expose its actions to the public.

Nechaev saw Ivanov as a traitor and laid plans to make an example of him. On December 3, 1869,

Nechaev and three members of the People's Revenge lured Ivanov to a quiet corner of a Moscow park. There, Nechaev strangled and then shot Ivanov. The group weighted the body with stones and threw it into a pond, where the police discovered it several days later.

Despite Nechaev's careful planning, the murder of Ivanov was easily solved by the authorities. The police found evidence that led them to Nechaev's accomplices, who were arrested. These men revealed many details of the People's Revenge. With the police after him, Nechaev fled Russia again to seek safe haven in Switzerland.

A public trial of Nechaev's helpers in the murder of Ivanov was held in Moscow. The men were found guilty and sentenced to exile in Siberia. The People's Revenge, with its leader in Switzerland and many of its members living thousands of miles from Moscow, ceased to exist.

Nechaev moved to Geneva, where he lived from January to July 1870. He continued writing revolutionary proclamations calling on soldiers, peasants, and workers to set fire to Russian cities and factories. Nechaev also wrote articles in anarchist journals throughout Europe. In one of these articles, he used a pseudonym and announced the death of Sergei Nechaev. As a dead revolutionary hero, Nechaev believed, he would gain new followers inside Russia. The report of his death might also put an end to the police search for him.

Nechaev's article, however, did not deceive the Russian government. The Third Section knew that Nechaev was alive and well in Switzerland. Still fearing his abilities as an organizer, the Russians asked the Swiss government to deport Nechaev. But many people in Switzerland—a traditional shelter for political refugees—opposed this demand.

At the same time, Nechaev was losing many of his Russian friends inside Switzerland. Mikhail Bakunin became a target of blackmail after Nechaev stole several letters from Bakunin's home. As word of Nechaev's methods circulated throughout Europe and Russia, he quickly lost support. Nechaev's allies were no longer willing to risk their lives and freedom to protect him.

The Third Section finally caught Nechaev in a Zurich cafe on August 14, 1872. Although he claimed to be a Serbian, the police soon discovered that Nechaev was unable to speak the Serbian language. After several days, the police found a witness who positively identified their prisoner as Nechaev.

The Swiss government now had a notorious revolutionary in custody. Swiss laws required the country to protect political refugees. Russian officials, however, claimed Nechaev was a common criminal whom they would put on trial for premeditated murder. They asked the Swiss to release Nechaev into their custody. Eventually, the Swiss complied with Russia's request and sent Nechaev back to his homeland.

As soon as Nechaev arrived in St. Petersburg, the

police imprisoned him. Later they sent him to Moscow, where he went on trial in January 1873. After five hours, the court found Nechaev guilty of murder and sentenced him to 20 years of exile and hard labor in Siberia.

In fact, the tsar and his officials had no intention of ever releasing Nechaev. Nor would they send this dangerous revolutionary to Siberia, a vast and distant region, where prisoners were under few restraints. Bakunin himself had escaped from Siberian exile. Unknown to the public and to most of the police, the tsarist officials sent Nechaev back to St. Petersburg and locked him up in the Peter and Paul fortress—the worst dungeon in Russia.

Nechaev lived in a small, dark, solitary cell in a wing of the fortress that held just one other prisoner. The government allowed him no contact with the outside world. He could write no letters and receive no visitors. At one point, after he caused trouble with the prison warden, the guards locked Nechaev in arm and leg irons for two years.

To most of the student revolutionaries who still lived in Russia, Nechaev was simply a convicted murderer who would probably never be heard from again. Many of Nechaev's ideas, however, survived his disappearance. In the 1870s, students in St. Petersburg formed a new terrorist organization called the People's Will. Members of this group carefully planned the assassination of Tsar Alexander II.

Through his forceful personality, Nechaev, in the meantime, converted several prison guards to his cause. During the 1870s, numerous assassination attempts against the tsar were taking place. Although the attempts failed, Nechaev convinced many of his jailers that the tsar's aides had joined him in a revolutionary plot. To help Nechaev, the guards smuggled in writing and reading materials.

In 1881, Nechaev managed to make contact with the People's Will. The members of the group, shocked to learn that Nechaev was still in St. Petersburg, made plans to free him from jail. The group would provide money, transportation, and a false passport. Nechaev and his accomplices outside the prison walls also plotted to capture the tsar and his family in the Peter and Paul fortress, where the Russian leader regularly attended services in a royal chapel.

Nechaev smuggled out new proclamations from his cell. He called for a revolutionary dictatorship and a reign of terror that would sweep away the government and destroy the ruling class in Russia. He also announced plans for a secret tribunal that would carry out summary executions of all those he considered traitors and spies.

On March 13, 1881, a member of the People's Will managed to assassinate the tsar by throwing a bomb at the royal carriage. The murder caused a violent reaction by the police and by the Third Section. Instead of rebelling, many Russians who were frightened by the

A bomb-throwing terrorist from the People's Will murdered Russia's Tsar Alexander II in 1881.

assassination praised the government's actions. The arrest of members of the People's Will after the tsar's death ended Nechaev's plans for escape.

While making their arrests, the police discovered that the tsar's assassins had been communicating with Nechaev. The government arrested the guards who had helped Nechaev inside the prison and assigned a new warden to watch over the famous terrorist. The warden reduced Nechaev's food rations and moved him into complete isolation. Nechaev developed scurvy, a painful disease that is caused by a poor diet. He died in November 1882.

Although the People's Will had murdered the tsar, the result that Nechaev had hoped for did not come to pass. A revolution did occur, but not until 1917, more than 30 years after Nechaev was put in his grave.

Many members of the People's Will were memorialized by the Soviet government that came to power in 1917. The tsar's assassins earned praise in newspapers and history books, and the Soviets named several streets in St. Petersburg after them. But the government gave no such honors to Nechaev. Rather than a street name, "Nechaev" became a part of the language. The Russian word *nechaevshchina* means to use any methods at hand—including murder and blackmail—to gain one's ends.

Before they became respected politicians, many national leaders—including Ireland's Michael Collins—had fought violently against colonial rule.

2

Michael Collins
and the Irish Republican Army

*A*t the hour of dusk in a late August evening, a small convoy moved along a country road in southwestern Ireland. Riding in open cars, Michael Collins and his guards were finishing a tour of inspection in County Cork. It was 1922. Now 31 years old and a leader of the Irish government, Collins had come a long way since his impoverished boyhood, which he had spent on a farm just a few miles from this lonely road.

Suddenly, bullets tore into the ground. Ordering his driver to stop, Collins jumped out of the car and took cover beside an armored truck. His guards began trading shots with gunmen in the surrounding hills.

A year before, the men firing at Collins in this ambush had been devoted to him. They were farmers

27

and workers ready to obey his commands and risk their lives for his cause. Now, after their leader had finally succeeded in a long and bitter struggle, they were determined to kill him.

The firefight lasted more than half an hour. As night fell, a bullet hit a nearby truck and ricocheted into the head of Michael Collins. Within a few minutes, Ireland's young leader lay dead on the ground.

Michael Collins was one of the founders of the modern Republic of Ireland. He organized one of the most effective guerrilla organizations in history—the Irish Republican Army (IRA). Under his leadership, the IRA fought for and won Irish independence from England. To the Irish who were demanding self-rule after centuries of domination by England, Collins was a man of great talent and courage. To the English, he was a bloodstained gangster—a terrorist.

Yet Collins lost his life, not to the English, but to members of his own organization. The IRA men who ambushed Collins saw him as a traitor for having signed a treaty that divided Ireland, leaving the northern six counties of Ulster under English rule.

The murder reflected a deep division among the Irish that continues to this day. The IRA itself has split into rival wings. Some IRA members are still fighting to unify southern and northern Ireland—even though a majority of Northern Ireland's people want to remain a part of the United Kingdom (which includes England, Scotland, and Wales). In the name of reunification, the

IRA now attacks civilians in both Ireland and England—a practice Michael Collins never would have permitted.

The English and the Irish have been in conflict in Ireland since the 16th century, when England began sending colonists to take possession of Irish land. English monarchs also tried to impose the Protestant branch of Christianity on the Irish, who are devout Roman Catholics. Over the centuries, the counties of northern Ireland became mostly Protestant. But most of the people in the rest of Ireland remained Catholic.

The French Revolution of the 1790s inspired many Irish leaders to fight for independence. A group known as the United Irishmen sought to break Ireland's ties with England and to create a republic. But their attempts failed. In 1801, under the Act of Union, Ireland became part of the United Kingdom of Great Britain and Ireland.

The Irish lived in extreme poverty during the 19th century. A famine killed more than one million Irish people in the 1840s. Many more left to seek a better life in North America. Irish leaders in the United States and Ireland formed secret societies to attack English interests in Ireland. One of these societies was the Irish Republican Brotherhood (IRB), which began in 1858.

IRB members were sworn to secrecy and pledged to fight for an independent Irish republic. These "republicans" used acts of violence to frighten English leaders into meeting their demands. In 1882, another secret society, the Invincible Brotherhood, murdered two English officials in Phoenix Park in Dublin. These acts and others brought reprisals from the English, but failed to win independence for the Irish.

For several decades after the Phoenix Park murders, the IRB gained little in their fight for independence. But in 1909, a new IRB fighter—Michael Collins— took the oath of membership.

Collins was born near Clonakilty, County Cork, in 1890. Like many Irish families, the Collinses were tenant farmers. They paid rent to an English landlord for the use of the land. Although the English government eventually allowed Irish tenants to buy their own farms, the Collins family and many others were too poor to purchase the land they farmed.

Michael Collins left home at 15 to take a job in London, England, as a postal clerk. In 1909, while still in England, he joined the IRB, which was made up of Irish clerks, farmers, and laborers. Not everyone in Ireland, however, supported the goals and methods of the IRB. Some Irish were Protestant and wanted their nation to remain a part of the United Kingdom. Many Catholics favored a limited form of self-rule that would keep Ireland under the English monarchy.

With few prospects at home, Collins and other Irish made their living in England. A skilled accountant, Collins worked for a time in a stockbroker's office. But when World War I began in 1914, England called up millions of men to fight against Germany. To escape the draft, Collins returned to his homeland.

After settling in Dublin, Collins began working actively for the republican cause. He joined the Irish Volunteers, a republican militia that was planning an armed rebellion in the Irish capital. On Easter Monday, April 24, 1916, Collins and other Volunteers seized Dublin's central post office. The leaders of the uprising proclaimed a free Irish republic.

The people of Dublin did not rally to the aid of the Volunteers. Within a few days, the English had stormed the post office and crushed the revolt. They sent Collins to Frongoch, a prison camp in Wales. The English also captured and executed 15 leaders of the Easter Rebellion.

After his release in December 1916, Collins returned to Dublin. He became a secretary for the National Aid, an organization that helped the families of men killed in the Easter Rebellion. The National Aid office was located two blocks from Dublin Castle— the headquarters of English forces in Ireland.

From this office, Collins organized the Volunteers and members of the IRB into a new underground movement. He gained a loyal following in Dublin, where many people—shocked by the executions after the Easter Rebellion—now opposed English rule. The threat of being drafted into the English army was also driving thousands of Irishmen to the republican side.

Although the IRB was gaining new members, the

British soldiers inspect the damage to Dublin's central post office during the Easter Rebellion of 1916.

organization needed weapons. Collins led operations to salvage arms from ships wrecked by German submarines off the Irish coast. From the National Aid office, Collins also set up a gunrunning network in England. The English eventually discovered Collins's operations and began searching for him.

To strike back at the republicans, the English hired Irish spies and began arresting IRB members. The government censored Irish newspapers, and heavily armed police took control of rebellious areas in the countryside. From his offices and hideouts in Dublin, Collins directed the small and scattered bands of IRB volunteers. He collected money for the organization and recruited farmers and townspeople to provide food and shelter to IRB members on the run.

Collins also became a member of *Sinn Féin*, a political party made up of Irish republicans. In 1918, he was elected to represent Ireland in the British Parliament. Like many other Irish politicians, however, Collins was under the threat of arrest and imprisonment. Instead of attending the British Parliament in London, he remained underground. The Sinn Féin leaders formed their own parliament—called the *Dáil Éireann*—and named Collins as minister of finance.

By 1919, English agents were searching high and low for Collins in the streets of Dublin. They arrested and interrogated many of his aides. England offered a cash reward of 10,000 pounds for his capture. Nevertheless, Collins moved openly about Dublin, making his rounds of the city on a bicycle. Not bothering to wear disguises, he bluffed his way past roadblocks and search parties by claiming to be a simple workingman or an English undercover agent. He escaped house searches by hiding under tables or fleeing into alleys from back doors. Despite several close calls, he was never captured.

Collins built up a large and efficient spy network that took orders directly from his office. Postal workers stole the mail from Dublin Castle—the English headquarters—and turned it over to the IRB. Ticket clerks at railway stations helped IRB fugitives travel to hiding places in remote areas of the country. Sailors and dockworkers in Ireland's ports helped Collins smuggle in needed guns and ammunition.

Collins also planted spies within Dublin Castle and turned many of the English over to his side. After World War I ended in November 1918, the English army sent troops, tanks, and armored cars into Dublin. But with only a few thousand men under arms and with most Irish now turning against them, the English could not break Collins's network.

In 1919, the Irish Volunteers became the Irish Republican Army (IRA). The IRA leaders organized the group into brigades and put these units under the direction of a headquarters staff in Dublin. Most IRA fighters went about their daily lives and met in the evening or on weekends to drill or undertake missions. Gradually, the IRA took control of Ireland's rural districts, while the English ran the cities and larger towns.

Determined to keep control of Ireland, the English tried to turn the Irish people against the republicans by accusing the IRA of terrorism. English newspapers ran sensational stories about attacks and assassinations arranged by Collins and the IRA leadership. English leaders called Collins a gangster and a bloody terrorist. In this way, England hoped to divide Collins and the other republicans from Irish politicians who favored keeping Ireland within the United Kingdom. A civil war between these two factions would help England keep its grip on Ireland.

In August 1919, the leaders of Sinn Féin had the

IRA take an oath of loyalty to the Dáil parliament. The oath was meant to unite the military and political wings of the Irish republicans. Three weeks later, the English banned all public meetings of the Dáil.

The violence in Dublin grew worse. Dublin Castle sent English agents known as *G-men* to hunt for IRA leaders. Collins responded by targeting many of the G-men for assassination. He organized the Dublin Brigade—also known as "The Squad"—to eliminate English spies. But the English were certain that their superior arms, training, and numbers would prevail.

In fact, Collins and the IRA were prepared for nearly every move the English agents made in Dublin. Collins had turned a Dublin Castle clerk named Ned Broy into an IRA spy. Broy, whom the English had hired as a typist, made copies of all reports signed by the G-men. He then turned the copies over to Collins. Many G-men writing and signing reports on IRA activities were, in fact, signing their own death warrants.

In 1920, the English declared martial law in Ireland. Dublin and other cities fell under a curfew. Anyone appearing on the streets after 10 P.M. could be arrested. To fight the IRA, the English brought in volunteers known as "Black-and-Tans." Named for their oddly colored uniforms, the Black-and-Tans were badly trained and unemployed war veterans and criminals. They had a reputation for cruelty, and the Irish people despised them.

On April 3, 1920, Collins and the IRA organized

Amid the 1920 unrest in Ireland, authorities frisk an IRA suspect at gunpoint.

their most popular action. IRA brigades fanned out across the countryside, burning tax offices and more than 300 empty police barracks.

In 1921, the British dispatched a team of experienced police agents to find Michael Collins. In response, Collins organized a coordinated strike. On a Sunday morning, the IRA hunted down and shot ten English agents.

The English panicked. On the day of the shootings, a team of G-men and officers was sent to a soccer match with orders to arrest as many IRA members as they could find. The search ended in a gunfight, in which 14 people died. Ever since, the Irish have commemorated this day as "Bloody Sunday."

After the killings, English leaders concluded that they would never regain control of Ireland. The English and the IRA signed a truce in July 1921. In December, the government offered a treaty to Collins and several other Dáil representatives. This agreement established the self-governing Irish Free State. Although the Irish Free State, like Canada, would be a member of the British dominion, English soldiers would leave Ireland. The six Protestant counties in the north—Ulster—would remain part of Great Britain.

Seeking to prevent more bloodshed, Michael Collins signed the treaty and later became the head of a provisional Irish government. But in August 1922, his compromise with the British cost him his life on a road in County Cork. For nine months after Collins's death, a civil war raged in Ireland between the new army of the Irish Free State and the IRA republicans who opposed the treaty.

The struggle among the Irish over the terms of the treaty continued for years, as Ireland's leaders gradually lessened their country's ties to the British Empire. In 1949, the Irish government declared the complete independence of the Republic of Ireland. The six counties of Ulster—Northern Ireland—remained a part of the United Kingdom.

Throughout these years, the IRA never ceased calling for the union of the Republic of Ireland and Ulster.

In the late 1950s, the IRA began raiding border posts between Northern Ireland and the Irish republic. In 1969, the IRA split into two wings—official and provisional. Members of the provisional IRA, known as the "Provos," began to press their demands with the use of violence.

The provisional IRA launched a terrorist campaign in 1970 to bring about the breakdown of law and order in Northern Ireland. Their goal was to force Britain to impose direct rule over Northern Ireland, which they hoped would cause an all-out revolt among the people of Ulster. In 1972, after bombings, riots, and assassinations, the IRA attained their goal. The British suspended the legislature of Northern Ireland and took direct control of the country's government.

IRA assassins, partially supplied and trained by Libya, also carried out a series of attacks in the 1970s and 1980s against prominent British leaders. Lord Mountbatten, a distinguished British war veteran, and Ross McWhirter, the publisher of the *Guinness Book of World Records*, died at the hands of the IRA. Margaret Thatcher, the British prime minister, narrowly escaped an IRA bombing in 1984.

The IRA gained the support of many Irish Catholics who want the British to leave Ulster. During the 1980s, the IRA was also effective in controlling some rural areas of Northern Ireland. Within these "no-go" areas, the British appeared only with armored car protection. The IRA also forced "donations" from local residents. The Provisionals replaced the regular court system with their own form of justice. Anyone found helping the British was quickly punished by execution or by "kneecapping"—being shot in the knees.

The IRA avoids head-on battles with the British army, which greatly outnumbers the Provos. Instead, the group relies on timed explosives and on hit-and-run shootings. Using grenades and mortars, they attack isolated convoys of British soldiers in the countryside. IRA gunmen also take part in parades and public demonstrations and attempt to turn them into bloody confrontations

To avoid arrest, IRA members never carry guns or explosives with them. Instead, the Provos keep their arms in hiding places. IRA leaders plan an operation and send for volunteers, who arrive in a "safe house." The planners then describe and locate the target—an individual, a vehicle, or a building. Volunteers pick up the clothing, guns, and ammunition they need for the mission. After carrying out their assignment, they return to the safe house to turn in the arms and clothing. The volunteers then return to their normal working lives. They carry nothing—no publications, identity cards, weapons, or clothing—that would connect them with the IRA.

The IRA stages dozens of attacks every year. Yet the killings within Northern Ireland became so routine during the 1970s and 1980s that many of them never were reported outside Great Britain. Occasionally, a deadly IRA attack will gain worldwide attention. In November 1987, an IRA bomb exploded in the Protestant Ulster village of Enniskillen, killing 11 people. The incident was captured on film and broadcast all over the world.

To gain more attention in the news media, the provisional IRA also carries out bombings in London. IRA bombs have exploded in London's department stores, railroad stations, and busy intersections. The organization has also attacked the home of Britain's prime minister with explosives fired from the street.

IRA bombings in Britain and in Ireland have prompted harsh reaction from the authorities. The British government has banned all media interviews or speeches of IRA or Sinn Féin members. The government has built British army bases that control traffic at several points along the border between Northern Ireland and the Republic of Ireland. A large force of troops and armored vehicles is stationed permanently in Northern Ireland, and the British maintain detention centers where they can hold suspected IRA terrorists without trial.

Many British officials hope that acts like the Enniskillen bombing will turn even Irish Catholics against the provisional IRA. For their part, the leaders of the IRA seek to make the British occupation of Ulster costly and unpopular. Some people in Britain want to compromise, but a withdrawal of British forces would probably lead to civil war between the Catholics and the Protestants of Northern Ireland. For this reason, the conflict in Northern Ireland is at a standoff.

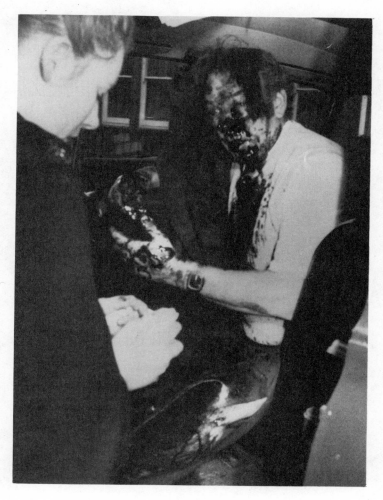

Five people were killed and many more injured in December 1983, when an IRA bomb exploded in London outside Harrod's department store. A policewoman helps one of the victims.

Armed with an AK-47 assault rifle, Yasir Arafat (left) walks with an aide during the Israeli siege of Beirut in June 1982.

3

Yasir Arafat and the
Palestine Liberation Organization

*B*oth Jews and Arabs claim their homeland in ancient Palestine, a narrow strip of territory in the Middle East between the Jordan River and the coast of the Mediterranean Sea. Both peoples also claim Jerusalem—the capital of the modern Jewish nation of Israel—as a site sacred to their religions. Their conflict, which dates back hundreds of years, has contributed greatly to one of the modern world's greatest fears—violent terrorism.

After winning World War I in 1918, Great Britain took control of Palestine. At that time, Arabs made up a majority of Palestine's population. But during the next few decades, Jews from Europe, North America, and Africa began arriving in the region. Driven from their homes by persecution, the Jews laid claim to Palestine. They dreamed of forming a democratic nation in the Middle East to which all Jews could immigrate.

For decades, violence took place among Arab residents, Jewish settlers, and the British occupation forces. Finally, in 1948, Britain withdrew from Palestine, leaving the Jews and the Arabs to fight a civil war. This ended in victory for the Jewish forces and the founding of Israel. Many of the Palestinian Arabs became refugees in the neighboring nations of Jordan, Lebanon, Syria, and Egypt.

The Palestinian Arabs had no nation, no government, and no leader. The Arab countries did not allow them to become citizens or to hold passports. But after the Arab-Israeli Six-Day War of 1967, one man emerged as the main Palestinian spokesman: Yasir Arafat. To many Arabs, Arafat became a hero. To the Israelis, and to much of the Western world, Arafat was simply a terrorist disguised as a politician.

Arafat has become one of the world's most familiar faces. He spends much of his time in public places, attending meetings with heads of state and important diplomats. Yet many of the events of his life, including his birth and childhood, are a mystery. Although he claims to have been born in Jerusalem, his family moved to Cairo, Egypt, before he was born in 1929. One of his teachers gave him the nickname of Yasir, which means "easygoing" in Arabic.

Arafat's childhood was an unhappy one. When he

was four, his mother died, and his father sent him away to live with an uncle in Jerusalem. In the 1930s, this city—a holy place for Muslims, Christians, and Jews—was under the control of Great Britain. For several years, Arafat lived near the Western Wall, a site sacred to the Jews.

Arafat's father was a member of the Muslim Brotherhood, a group that believed in strict observance of Islamic religious law. As a boy, Arafat was influenced by his father and by many other strong-willed Muslim leaders. One of these was the head of Jerusalem's Muslim population, Haj Amin al-Husseini, who organized the Muslims in Palestine to fight both the British and the Jews for control of the region. After the British withdrew from Palestine in 1948, Arafat joined a Muslim Brotherhood guerrilla unit to fight the new nation of Israel.

With the Arab defeat in the war, Arafat moved to Gaza, a small strip of land between Israel and Egypt. He joined guerrilla attacks on Jewish forces as well as on Palestinians who disagreed with his objectives. Feuds among the many small Arab guerrilla groups, however, prevented them from doing much damage.

In 1950, Arafat moved back to Cairo and enrolled in the engineering program at King Fuad (later Cairo) University. Although he was indifferent to his academic work, Arafat had a great talent for organizing and leading the Palestinian Arabs who were studying in Egypt. In 1955, the Palestinians elected him president of their student association, the General Union of Palestinian Students.

In 1957, while Arafat was in eastern Europe, a plot against Gamal Abdel Nasser, president of Egypt, had been discovered. Suspecting Arafat of taking part in the plot, the Egyptian government arrested him after he returned from Europe. Arafat spent two months in an Egyptian jail. Then he left for Kuwait, a small nation on the Persian Gulf.

With his knowledge of engineering, Arafat started a construction company in Kuwait. The country was growing rich from the sale of its oil, and construction projects were keeping thousands of Palestinian laborers

In the 1950s and 1960s, Egyptian President Gamal Abdel Nasser (waving) emerged as the leading spokesman for Arab nationalism, which included the Palestinian cause.

busy. Arafat made contacts in the Kuwaiti administration and landed large contracts for work in the country's capital city.

Although his business was successful, Arafat spent much of his time and money on organizing Palestinians. With several close friends, he began the Palestine Liberation Committee. Later the name of the committee was changed to *Fatah*, an Arabic word meaning victory. Fatah's goal was the defeat of the Jews and the armed reconquest of Israel, which the Arabs still called Palestine. Fatah printed a small newsletter called *Our Palestine* and distributed it to Palestinians in Europe and the Middle East. Fatah's leaders used *Our Palestine* to recruit new members outside Kuwait.

Arafat sold his company in 1963 and moved from Kuwait to Syria. The Syrian government allowed Fatah to set up training camps on its territory, which borders Israel. From these camps, guerrillas crossed into Israel to raid settlements and to destroy irrigation equipment.

Arab leaders, however, viewed the Palestinian raids with alarm. Bombings carried out by guerrillas risked retaliation by the Israelis, and Egypt and Syria had no desire to fight another war with Israel. To gain some control over the Palestinians, President Nasser of Egypt founded the Palestine Liberation Organization (PLO) in 1964. Arafat did not join the PLO, however. He and other Fatah leaders considered it to be no more than a weak puppet of the Arab nations.

In the mid-1960s, guerrilla raids by Fatah and other

groups steadily raised tensions in the Middle East. From the West Bank—a part of Jordan—and from Gaza, Palestinians were crossing into Israel and planting bombs in restaurants, movie theaters, and other public places. The Israelis, in turn, raided Palestinian villages in Syria and Jordan, killing civilians and bulldozing private homes.

The new, modern weapons sold to Egypt and Syria by the Soviet Union led these nations to believe they could defeat Israel. In the spring of 1967, Syria began shelling Israel from the Golan Heights, which lay along Israel's northeastern border. Soon afterward, Egypt blocked Israeli ships from reaching their home ports. On June 5, Israel struck back. It destroyed the Egyptian air force in a massive air raid and, within a few days, defeated the armies of Jordan and Syria. Israel seized the West Bank, the Golan Heights, Gaza, and the Sinai Peninsula, an Egyptian territory.

Despite all the talk about fighting for Palestine, the PLO had taken no part in the Six-Day War. Because of this, the organization's leaders lost their prestige among the Palestinians, who saw that the PLO and the Arab governments were interested only in keeping the Palestinian movement under their control. Arab leaders, demoralized by their defeat, now took very little interest in solving the problems of the Palestinians.

Fatah's leaders met to decide what to do. Some favored disbanding the group and giving up on the reconquest of Palestine. Arafat, however, vowed to fight on with the new generation of Palestinian refugees created by the Six-Day War. After convincing his comrades to join him, Arafat was named Fatah's official spokesman.

In 1968, Israel mounted a full-scale attack on the refugee camp at Karameh near the Jordan River. Although they had plenty of time to leave the village, Arafat and several hundred Fatah fighters decided to stand their ground. Armed with rifles and grenades, the guerrillas fought Israeli tanks to a standstill. To the Palestinians, Karameh became a powerful symbol of resistance—and Arafat became a hero.

After Karameh, Arafat gained the support of Nasser. The Egyptian president urged Arafat to bring Fatah into the PLO. In June 1968, the PLO was reorganized to include Arafat's organization. Fatah members now made up a majority of the PLO's governing committee. In February 1969, this committee elected Arafat as the PLO chairman.

Many groups besides Fatah were now PLO members. The Popular Front for the Liberation of Palestine (PFLP), headed by a Palestinian doctor named George Habash, favored a Communist revolution in the Middle East. Habash opposed Arafat's dealings with moderate Arab nations like Jordan. PFLP guerrillas had no wish to settle in the West Bank or in Gaza and no desire to live out their lives in refugee camps in Lebanon or Jordan. They wanted nothing less than a complete defeat of Israel.

In 1968, the PFLP began a campaign of terrorism to focus the world's attention on Palestinian grievances. Hijackings, kidnappings, and assassinations took place in the Middle East and in Europe. The PFLP killed or injured innocent civilians unlucky enough to be in the wrong place at the wrong time. Habash argued that terrorism was the only weapon available to the Palestinians and the only way to retaliate for Israel's occupation of Arab lands.

In 1969 and 1970, under Arafat's direction, the PLO continued its guerrilla raids on Israel from the camps in Jordan. These raids brought fierce retaliation from Israeli forces. As the violence worsened, King Hussein, the leader of Jordan, saw his country slipping out of control.

The final straw came in September 1970, when Palestinian terrorists hijacked three commercial airliners and forced them to land in the Jordanian desert. When the terrorists evacuated the passengers and then blew up the planes on the ground, Hussein lost face in front of the entire world. Powerless to stop a terrorist act on Jordanian soil, he seemed to be losing control of his own country to Arafat's organization. To retaliate, King Hussein ordered the Jordanian army to drive the PLO out of Jordan.

For days, a battle raged between the Jordanians and the PLO. Thousands of fighters died on both sides. In the end, the lightly armed guerrillas of the PLO proved to be no match for Jordan's troops, planes, and tanks.

Disguised as an Arab sheik, Arafat fled for his life from Jordan.

The PLO scattered. Some guerrillas moved to Syria; others went to southern Lebanon. Refugee camps in southern Lebanon and in the Lebanese capital of Beirut became the PLO's home during the 1970s. A group of Fatah guerrillas headed by Arafat's deputy, Salah Khalaf, founded a new terrorist group, Black September, to take revenge for the defeat in Jordan. The group's first act was the assassination of a Jordanian ambassador in 1971.

In September 1972, Black September attacked the residence of an Israeli team at the Olympic Games in Munich, West Germany. The group took the athletes hostage and demanded the release of 200 Palestinian prisoners being held by Israel. By attacking the most popular sporting event in the world, Black September had gained a worldwide television audience for its action.

The German government negotiated with the group and allowed Black September to move to a nearby airport. The hostages were held captive in a helicopter as negotiations continued. At the airport, however, the German police attacked the terrorists, killing several of them. Before the battle was over, the Palestinians had opened fire on the Israeli athletes and killed nine of them.

Arafat claimed to have little control over these terrorist actions. He considered himself a diplomat with

In Munich, an Olympic official bargains with a Black September terrorist (left).

the difficult task of controlling violent radicals within his own organization. In 1973, Fatah and Arafat announced that they were opposed to further terrorism outside of what they called Palestine.

Raids on Israeli targets continued. In 1974, the PFLP attacked the Israeli settlement of Kiryat Shimoneh. Terrorists burst into houses and apartment buildings, spraying the inhabitants with machine gun fire and throwing hand grenades. In the same year, terrorists raided a school in Ma'alot, Israel, and murdered 16 students.

At the same time, Arafat was gaining respect in the diplomatic world. After the Arab-Israeli conflict known as the 1973 Yom Kippur War, Arafat declared that he

Terrorist raids, such as the April 1980, attack on the children's dormitory at Kibbutz Misgav-Am, prompted the Israeli government to remove the PLO from Lebanon.

was in favor of a separate Palestinian homeland in territories occupied by Israel since the Six-Day War. This position, which implied Arafat's acceptance of an Israeli state, made new enemies for the PLO chairman among many Palestinian terrorists. In 1974, however, the United Nations invited him to speak before them in New York.

With no government in control of southern Lebanon, Arafat's PLO gained direct control over many

Lebanese villages and ports. The PLO also controlled several neighborhoods in Beirut.

Raids across the Lebanese-Israeli border became common in the late 1970s and early 1980s. In retaliation for the attacks, Israel invaded Lebanon in 1982 and drove the PLO and Arafat out of the country. Jordan, Syria, and Egypt did nothing to help. Since the invasion, Arafat has made his headquarters in Tunis, Tunisia—more than a thousand miles from Palestine.

During the 1980s, Arafat continued his diplomacy for the PLO. He traveled to meet any king or president who would give him the opportunity to present his case. But as Palestinians grew more frustrated in their quest for a homeland, many turned away from the PLO and from its leader.

In December 1987, anger and frustration among Palestinians in the West Bank and Gaza erupted into violence. Young Palestinians set tires ablaze and attacked Israeli police with stones and gasoline bombs. Arabs called these events the *intifadeh*—an uprising.

Taken by surprise, the PLO attempted to control and direct the intifadeh. PLO leaders sent instructions to the West Bank and Gaza by telephone and fax. But many young Palestinians paid little heed to Arafat and looked to more militant groups for leadership.

In 1988, Arafat declared that he was ready to recognize Israel and was prepared to negotiate with Israeli representatives for a Palestinian homeland. Although Israel continued to denounce the PLO as a terrorist

During the intifadeh, an Arafat follower stands defiant in a West Bank village.

group, these actions—and the continuing violence of the intifadeh—put pressure on Israel to make a deal with the Palestinians.

Just as the intifadeh began to lose momentum, another conflict arose in the Middle East—this time in Arafat's former home of Kuwait. In the summer of 1990, Saddam Hussein, the leader of Iraq, ordered his army to invade Kuwait.

Saddam claimed to be fighting for the Palestinian cause and refused to pull his forces out of Kuwait. Palestinians in the West Bank and Gaza, believing Saddam had a chance to defeat Israel as well, demonstrated in favor of Iraq. Arafat, attempting to keep his control over the militant Palestinians, publicly praised Iraq's actions.

For this, many of the wealthy Persian Gulf nations ended their support of the PLO. Iraq's powerful army and air force posed a threat to these poorly defended states and to their valuable oil reserves.

In early 1991, forces from the United States, Europe, and several Arab countries drove Iraq from Kuwait. For the PLO and Arafat, supporting Saddam

Although Arafat has lost much of his popularity, he remains a hero to many Palestinians, including this West Bank boy holding his picture.

turned out to be a serious mistake. Palestinians living and working in Kuwait lost their jobs and were forced to flee the country. Arafat lost face among the Arab rulers who had been supporting him. In Kuwait, Saudi Arabia, and other nations on the Persian Gulf, he was no longer a welcome guest.

The Palestinians had suffered another setback. But Iraqi missiles had fallen on Israel as well as on Saudi Arabia, and the short but violent war prompted a reopening of negotiations between Palestinian and Israeli diplomats—without Yasir Arafat.

Arafat has surprised the world by surviving these violent conflicts while many of his closest friends and colleagues have been killed in combat or assassinated. In April 1992, he survived a serious plane crash in Libya. Although Israel will not negotiate directly with the PLO, Arafat has remained the Palestinians' leader and spokesman. And while Arafat now lives far from Palestine, many Palestinians as well as many Israelis believe that no agreement between these two peoples is possible without his approval.

Scotland Yard, the British police agency, issued this 1975 photograph of the wanted and extremely dangerous Venezuelan terrorist Ilich Ramirez Sanchez—"Carlos."

4

Ilich Ramirez Sanchez
"Carlos"

*M*ost terrorists seek to achieve a political goal. The members of the IRA and the PLO, for example, have used terrorism to fight what they see as an unfair occupation of their lands. Others use terrorism to provoke a harsh government reaction—one that might cause a revolution. Most terrorists also have a personal stake in meeting their goals. They seek publicity or power. Through violence and fear, they hope to influence people and governments. This is why they choose a life of such great risk.

An exception was the Venezuelan terrorist Ilich Ramirez Sanchez, who was known to many as "Carlos." A sophisticated and educated man—but also a ruthless criminal—Carlos could easily have lived a peaceful life.

He had money and good family connections, and little need for bloodshed. He engaged in terrorism not out of political belief or ambition, but for the sake of adventure.

"Carlos" was born in 1949 as Ilich Ramirez Sanchez. He was the son of Altagracia Ramirez, a lawyer from San Cristóbal, Venezuela. Ramirez favored left-wing politics and was sympathetic to Latin America's many revolutionary movements. He named his three sons Vladimir, Ilich, and Lenin, after the communist founder of the Soviet Union—one of history's most famous revolutionaries.

In 1966, when he was 17, Ilich moved with his mother and two brothers to London, where the boys attended private schools. Two years later, his father helped him gain admittance to Patrice Lumumba Friendship University. This institute in Moscow, then the capital of the Soviet Union, instructed young men and women from Asia, Africa, and Latin America. Most of the students were members of the Communist parties in their home countries.

The university was also a recruiting center for the KGB—the Soviet Union's secret police organization. The KGB enlisted promising foreign students and sent them back home to work as political activists—or as spies. Many believe that the KGB brought Ilich Ramirez Sanchez into its ranks during his stay in Moscow.

Although Ilich was a good student, he quickly ran

into trouble with school authorities. He showed little respect for his teachers and missed important political meetings. The school suspended Ilich for "riotous behavior" after he joined a noisy street demonstration in Moscow. If the KGB was recruiting Ilich, however, this punishment may have been a cover story arranged by the university. After his suspension, Ilich returned to London.

Ilich had met many Palestinian students while in Moscow and had become interested in the Palestinian cause. To him, the Middle East was where the action was. Political turmoil and conflict in the region were making daily headlines in the newspapers. The future "Carlos" had a taste for undercover operations—and for violence.

After returning to Patrice Lumumba Friendship University in February 1970, Ilich contacted members of the Popular Front for the Liberation of Palestine (PFLP). But his behavior in Moscow grew even worse, and in June 1970, the university expelled him. Instead of returning to London, however, Ramirez Sanchez immediately traveled to a PFLP camp in Jordan.

George Habash had founded the PFLP after the Six-Day War in 1967 between Israel and the Arab countries. Habash opposed Yasir Arafat's intention to negotiate with Israel over the occupied territories of the West Bank and the Gaza Strip. Rather than negotiate, Habash and several other groups formed a "Rejection Front" of Palestinian groups based in Jordan that would

George Habash, leader of the Popular Front for the Liberation of Palestine (PFLP), trained as a doctor, but his acts of terrorism have been deadly.

continue the armed struggle against the Israelis. The PFLP became one of the largest and fastest-growing commando groups within the Rejection Front.

Habash's aide Wadi Haddad was one of the first Palestinian leaders to organize terrorist actions against European countries. In the late 1960s, Haddad planned a series of airline hijackings and bombings to gain both ransom money and publicity for the PFLP. Haddad's hijackings, which were carried out on Jordanian territory, greatly embarrassed King Hussein, Jordan's ruler. Eventually, instead of helping the Palestinian cause,

Haddad's actions led to open warfare between the Palestinians and the Jordanian army.

Haddad sought Westerners for his terrorist actions. He found willing volunteers in Europe, where many students supported the Palestinian cause. The PFLP invited these students to their camps in the Middle East. The organization trained some of them to carry out attacks in Europe. In 1969, a group of British volunteers working for the PFLP planted several bombs in the city of London.

Ilich Ramirez Sanchez arrived in Jordan in the summer of 1970. There he met Wadi Haddad, who had heard about the Venezuelan student from PFLP contacts in Moscow. After moving to Lebanon, Ilich went through intensive training in the use of explosives and weapons. Then he returned to Europe, using a phony Peruvian passport made by the PFLP. The passport carried his picture with the name of "Carlos Martinez." Using the passport, "Carlos" moved to Paris, where he joined a PFLP cell led by Mohammad Boudia.

Boudia was an exile from Algeria. Although he was known among friends as the manager of a theater company, he led a secret life as the leader of the PFLP's European operations. Boudia recruited several Europeans and had once used a group of French citizens to smuggle explosives into Israel. The plan had called for these "tourists" to bomb important hotels in the Israeli city of Tel Aviv. But the operation failed when Israeli police arrested Boudia's agents at the Tel Aviv airport.

In 1972, Boudia led a team of saboteurs into Trieste, Italy, where they set off a massive explosion at an oil refinery. In the summer of that year, Palestinian terrorists murdered several Israeli athletes at the Munich Olympics. Although Boudia was not involved in this action, it led to his own death.

To avenge the killings at Munich, the Israelis sent hit teams into Europe to attack any known Palestinian terrorists and, in particular, anyone connected with the operation at Munich. In June 1973, one of these teams planted a bomb in Boudia's car. The explosion blew Boudia into pieces and made Carlos the new leader of the PFLP's European organization.

After Boudia's death, Carlos received instructions directly from Wadi Haddad. First, Carlos was to close down Schonau, a transit camp set up in Austria for Jews emigrating from the Soviet Union. Thousands of emigrants had arrived at Schonau on their way to new homes in Israel. At the time of Boudia's death, the PFLP operation against Schonau had been in the planning stage for months. Members of Black September— the group that carried out the Munich massacre—had already been arrested in Austria while spying on Schonau.

Carlos came up with a new plan. On September 28, two terrorists boarded a train near the Austrian border, entered one of the passenger compartments, and took five Jews hostage. At the town of Marchegg, the terrorists took the captives off the train and boarded a truck for the airport at Vienna, the capital of Austria. The terrorists presented their demands, threatening to kill the hostages if their instructions were not followed.

Early on the morning of September 29, the Austrian government announced that the Schonau camp would be closed down and that the terrorists would be allowed to leave the country. The Austrian decision led Carlos, several years later, to plan another raid in Austria that would prove to be his last, and most spectacular, terrorist act.

In October 1973, Carlos traveled to London, where he set up a network of safe houses for his organization. The PFLP used these safe houses to hide arms, to take shelter from the police, if necessary, and to plan operations. To create the network, Carlos sought out girlfriends in the clubs and restaurants of London. One of these was a Spanish-speaking waitress named Maria Otaola. After gaining her confidence, Carlos used Otaola's apartment as a safe house. There he kept a locked bag of explosives and arms that he could retrieve whenever necessary. Friends who stopped by the apartment—and Maria Otaola herself—were not allowed to touch the bag and had no idea what it contained.

In February 1974, Carlos returned to Paris. His real identity was still unknown to his friends and to the police. But he had become the most important member of the PFLP working in Europe. He organized shipments of firearms to other terrorist groups in Europe and controlled the organization's finances. In Paris, a

PFLP courier named Michel Moukarbal became one of Carlos's close and trusted aides.

Carlos and the PFLP cell he headed did not operate in isolation. The organization had ties to several other terrorist groups, including the Japanese Red Army. In 1972, with the cooperation of the PFLP, this group had carried out a massacre at the Tel Aviv airport. Three Japanese Red Army members had opened fire with hand grenades and submachine guns in the middle of a crowded hall. The terrorists managed to kill more than 20 people before airport security stopped them.

Two years later, French police arrested one of the Japanese Red Army leaders, Suzuki Furuya, at Orly, an airport near Paris. Soon afterward, the Japanese terrorists called on the PFLP. As a payback for their massacre in Israel, they asked for the PFLP's help in getting Furuya released from his French prison.

Carlos planned a new operation in the summer of 1974 to get Furuya out. Instead of trying a prison break, however, he arranged an attack on the French government. On September 11, he set off for The Hague, the capital of the Netherlands. There he carefully observed the French embassy and made detailed plans of its security arrangements. He then collected the necessary weapons from a safe house in Paris. Two days later, three Japanese gunmen stormed the embassy building and took nine hostages, including the French ambassador. The terrorists demanded the release of Furuya and a large ransom payment.

Workers clean up the blood-stained floor of Tel Aviv's Ben-Gurion Airport in the aftermath of the Japanese Red Army attack.

French officials brought Furuya to the Netherlands on a plane and began negotiations. But the governments of France and the Netherlands could not agree on terms, and after two days, the embassy was still under siege. It was a standoff, and with the passage of time, the terrorists were losing the advantage.

Carlos returned to France, planning to hurry the negotiations along. One September afternoon, he entered Le Drugstore, a small area of shops and restaurants owned by a Jewish businessman. Standing on a balcony that overlooked the shops, Carlos tossed a hand grenade down into a crowd of people standing near a newsstand. The explosion killed two people and injured more than 34 others.

67

French police and firemen move people away from the injured victims of Carlos's 1974 bombing in Paris.

Soon afterward, Furuya was released. After allowing their hostages to leave the French embassy, the Japanese terrorists left the Netherlands safely on a plane supplied by the French. Carlos had once again faced down a powerful European government.

In June 1975, the true identity of Carlos was still unknown to the French police. The DST, the French national police agency, knew that a terrorist cell was operating in Paris, but had been unable to disrupt it. Carlos freely planned terrorist operations and could move around the French capital with little fear of being arrested. Yet he still depended on assistants who knew of his identity and his activities. One of these was

Michel Moukarbal, the Lebanese who had become Carlos's aide in Paris.

On June 11, Lebanese police arrested Moukarbal while he was trying to leave Lebanon on a flight to Paris. The police interrogated and then released him. He had denied any involvement with terrorist activities, but a search of his luggage had turned up a list of known terrorists. The Lebanese police contacted the French police, who prepared to follow Moukarbal as soon as he arrived in France. Within two days after landing in Paris, Moukarbal made a fatal mistake—he met in public with Carlos.

Suspecting that Moukarbal was being followed, Carlos decided to avoid further contact with him. He ordered Moukarbal to leave the city, while he took cover in a friend's apartment in a Paris street known as the Rue Toullier.

Rather than arrest Moukarbal, the DST followed him in the hopes of finding his boss in Paris. They allowed Moukarbal to walk the streets freely, but when he attempted to fly to England, he got only as far as Heathrow airport outside London. The British police stopped him and ordered him to fly back to France. Finally, on June 23, the DST arrested Moukarbal.

During the next few days, Moukarbal revealed to the DST his acquaintance with Carlos, although he denied being a terrorist. Finally, on June 27, he agreed to accompany three DST agents to the apartment in Rue Toullier. The agents, who at the time did not know Carlos's true identity, arrived at the apartment unarmed.

Carlos believed he was safe in the apartment in the Rue Toullier. Nevertheless, he had packed his bags and hidden his weapons in the bathroom in case he needed to escape the city. At about 9:40 P.M., the police arrived. When Carlos opened the door and saw Moukarbal with the DST agents, he suspected a trap. Excusing himself to the bathroom, he came out a few seconds later firing a powerful automatic pistol. His first target was Moukarbal, whom he instantly killed. He then murdered the two policemen.

Within a few days of the killings, the identity of Carlos was revealed in England. To avoid arrest, his friends in London had told a newspaper about the weapons and papers they had found in the bag Carlos had left in Maria Otaola's apartment. A nationwide manhunt was underway in France.

Carlos managed to slip through the net in Europe and return to the Middle East. Yet his career in Europe was not over. In the autumn of 1975, a few months after his return to the Middle East, PFLP leaders and Carlos planned a raid on a meeting of OPEC (the Organization of Petroleum Exporting Countries) in Vienna, Austria.

George Habash and Wadi Haddad saw many of the OPEC countries as their enemies. Saudi Arabia, Kuwait, Oman, and other OPEC members were wealthy Arab states that supported a moderate policy towards Israel. By taking OPEC's oil ministers hostage, the PFLP would gain worldwide attention for their cause as well as a large ransom from the OPEC nations.

Carlos entered Austria with five companions early in the morning of December 21, 1975. The group brought weapons across the border in a separate car, which met them outside the Austrian capital. Later that morning, the small band burst into the OPEC offices in Vienna, killing a security guard, a bodyguard, and one of the OPEC ministers. After entering a large conference room, the terrorists fired their weapons into the ceiling.

A brief firefight ensued in the corridor outside the conference room between the terrorists and a team of Austrian commandos, who had managed to enter the building. But Carlos and his comrades had wired explosives to the walls and the windows, and the only passage to the conference room was a long, empty corridor. Anyone attempting to storm the room would be shot before reaching the end of the hall. The situation was a stalemate.

While the OPEC ministers waited, Carlos produced a list of demands to be read over Austrian radio: The great oil wealth of the OPEC countries must, from now on, be used to advance the struggle of the Palestinians in the Middle East; the hostages would be executed if the statement was not broadcast; OPEC must provide a bus to take the terrorists and several hostages to the airport and a plane to take them out of the country. As they had during the Schonau raid, Austria's leaders accepted Carlos's demands.

The Austrians convinced the Algerian government to accept the terrorists and their prisoners. Carlos decided to bring with him 42 hostages, including 12 ministers and their staffs. The Austrians provided a bus and, at the airport, made ready a DC-9 airplane and a crew.

The plane flew to Algiers, the capital of Algeria. There Carlos allowed several oil ministers to leave the plane and go free. Fifteen hostages remained. After waiting several hours, Carlos instructed the pilot to fly to Tripoli, the capital of Libya.

After landing in Libya, Carlos sent one of his comrades into the control tower to negotiate. A new and much simpler demand was made: the governments of Iran and Saudi Arabia must pay for the release of their oil ministers. A few hours later, Carlos ordered the

At the Vienna airport, Austrian officials stand between one terrorist (boarding the airplane with a submachine gun) and another, believed to be Carlos (next to the bus).

72

pilot to fly back to Algiers. At the same time, a bank in Switzerland transferred a large amount of money—rumored to be several million dollars—to a bank in Aden, the capital of South Yemen. Aden was also a headquarters for Wadi Haddad and the PFLP. In Algiers, Carlos received word, through the Algerian government, that Wadi Haddad had received the ransom money from the Swiss banks.

Immediately, Carlos released the remaining hostages. The terrorists surrendered their weapons and left the airport. A convoy escorted Carlos into Algiers. He was never heard from again.

Many stories have circulated about the fate of Ilich Ramirez Sanchez, or "Carlos." He may be living in Libya, where Colonel Muammar Qaddafi has provided money, arms, and shelter to several terrorist groups. He may be somewhere else in the Middle East, where a friendly government is allowing him to enjoy the ransom money gained from his OPEC raid. He may be in southern Lebanon or Yemen with the PFLP. He may be in Moscow, where he received his education at the expense of the Soviet Union. Or he may be dead.

But as one of most wanted men in Europe, and one whose face, name, and history are well known, Carlos is no longer free to travel. To the relief of governments around the world, his career as a terrorist is almost certainly over.

Arab terrorists under Abu Nidal killed 13 people and injured 50 in their Rome airport massacre on December 27, 1985. The body of one gunman (far left, marked A) lies among the dead.

5

Abu Nidal

*L*eonardo da Vinci Airport, one of the busiest in Europe, lies 20 miles outside of Rome, Italy. Every day, thousands of travelers pass through the airport on their way to vacations and appointments. The Rome airport is an important link between Europe and the Middle East, and the national airlines of all the Middle Eastern countries have offices there.

Like many other airports, Leonardo da Vinci is especially crowded during the Christmas holiday season. On December 27, 1985, the airport corridors were bustling. In the departure hall, passengers checked their baggage and confirmed their seats on waiting planes. Although it was early in the morning, dozens of people were already lined up at ticket counters for Pan Am and for El Al—the national airline of Israel.

Unnoticed, four men moved from the airport entrance into the departure hall. They walked toward the El Al ticket counter and drew small submachine guns from underneath their coats. Shouting in Arabic, they opened fire and threw hand grenades into the crowd. Thousands of people dove underneath tables and chairs to take cover from the explosions and gun-fire.

Security guards rushed into the hall and opened fire on the terrorists. Three of the attackers died, and the guards took a fourth man prisoner. But it was too late to save several civilians who lay dead on the blood-spattered floor. The airport was filled with the screams of frightened travelers, many on the floor and many others running through exit doors and away from the terminal.

The attack came at a time when political violence was frightening travelers all over the world. Terrorists were hijacking planes, killing diplomats, and murdering civilians. Conflict and bloodshed in the Middle East made the headlines nearly every day. Yet the attack at Rome and another at Vienna, Austria, that occurred on the same day were especially shocking.

Most terrorist actions had a clear purpose. The terrorists at Leonardo da Vinci Airport, however, seemed to be killing for no reason. The gunmen had made no demands. They were Palestinians who simply targeted El Al—an Israeli company—and committed a massacre. The Palestinian people gained nothing. Italy and Austria, in fact, were two European countries that strongly supported Palestinian demands for a homeland in the Middle East. Soon, the world would learn that Abu Nidal was responsible.

Abu Nidal was born in 1937 as Sabri Khalil al-Banna. The al-Banna family was one of the wealthiest Arab families in Palestine. Khalil al-Banna, Sabri's father, owned large orange groves near the town of Jaffa, on the coast of the Mediterranean Sea. He had 11 children by his wife, and one—the youngest—by his maid. This illegitimate child would become the terrorist Abu Nidal.

Khalil al-Banna died in 1945. Rejected by many members of his family, Sabri dropped out of elementary school. In 1948, the year of the founding of the Jewish state of Israel, the al-Bannas suffered another misfortune. After Israel's victory over Arab armies in that year, many of the Arab residents of Jaffa lost their homes and property.

Thousands of Palestinian Arabs were fleeing Israel for neighboring countries, including Jordan, Lebanon, and Egypt. Those who had no place to stay took shelter in refugee camps. Sabri al-Banna and his brothers and sisters fled to the al-Burj camp in the Gaza Strip, a small territory that Egypt controlled. Later, the al-Bannas moved to Nablus, an Arab town on the West Bank of the Jordan River. In the 1950s, the West Bank was part of the kingdom of Jordan.

Without an education or relatives who could offer him a good job, Sabri al-Banna had to take poorly paid work to survive. Although he was a hard worker, his situation made him bitter and vengeful. Along with many others, he wanted the Palestinians to fight again for an Arab state in what had become Israel.

Many political movements formed in Arab countries in the 1950s sought the reconquest of Palestine. One of these was the Ba'ath party, which began in the 1950s in Syria. The Ba'athists worked to unite all Arabs in the Middle East and to destroy Israel. In 1955, Sabri al-Banna joined them.

The Ba'ath attacked any Arab ruler who favored negotiations with Israel. One of their favorite targets was King Hussein, the ruler of Jordan. In 1957, the Ba'athists mounted a violent uprising against Hussein in Amman, the Jordanian capital. The king put down this revolt and ordered his police to arrest members of the Ba'ath party. Sabri al-Banna escaped the police, but soon moved from the West Bank to Saudi Arabia.

This wealthy kingdom, which possessed enormous oil reserves, had become a land of opportunity for many Palestinians. The Saudi capital of Riyadh supported Palestinian laborers and traders. Here Sabri al-Banna opened his own electrical contracting business. Although he was successful, his politics had not changed. In Riyadh, he founded his own militant party, the Palestine Secret Organization.

In 1957, Yasir Arafat and others in Kuwait, another oil-rich country, formed Fatah, a Palestinian militia. While al-Banna worked to organize Palestinians in

Riyadh, Arafat was gaining a loyal following in Kuwait, Saudi Arabia, and in many other Arab countries where displaced Palestinians were settling. The Arab nations of the Middle East, however, sought to keep the various Palestinian groups under their control. To achieve this, President Nasser of Egypt and several other Arab leaders founded the Palestine Liberation Organization (PLO) in 1964.

Three years later, the Arabs and the Israelis went to war. The Palestinians believed that their moment had come—that Israel would be defeated and become the Arab nation of Palestine. But the war was a total defeat for Syria, Jordan, Egypt, and the Palestinian Arabs. Israel seized the West Bank and the Gaza Strip. Having lost the West Bank, the Palestinian guerrilla groups moved east of the Jordan River, where they set up camps and staged hit-and-run attacks on Israeli villages.

During the 1967 war, the Saudi government expelled several militants, including Sabri al-Banna, who were causing trouble among the kingdom's Palestinians. With Nablus and the West Bank under Israeli occupation, al-Banna went to Amman, the capital of Jordan. There he joined Arafat's Fatah and changed his name to Abu Nidal— which means "father of the struggle" in Arabic.

Abu Nidal rose quickly within Fatah. He founded a new trading company that Fatah used as a business front. Fatah held meetings in the company's offices and paid and received money through the company's bank accounts. Abu Nidal, who had a good head for business, won a growing respect from Fatah's leaders.

Yasir Arafat became chairman of the PLO in 1969. With thousands of guerrillas in its ranks, Fatah was the largest faction within the PLO. By this time, Abu Nidal felt himself to be an important member of the PLO and the equal of Arafat. In 1969, Abu Nidal persuaded the PLO leaders to appoint him as their official representative in Khartoum, the capital of the African country of Sudan.

In Sudan, Abu Nidal made contact with government officials on behalf of the PLO. But his stay in Khartoum did not last long. In early 1970, he returned to Amman, where conflict was brewing between the PLO and the Jordanian government. King Hussein feared an Israeli attack if PLO guerrillas continued their raids into Israel from Jordanian territory. Hussein also feared the growing power of the PLO, which controlled several bases within Jordan. Some Palestinians were speaking openly of overthrowing the king and establishing a Palestinian state in Jordan.

When he realized that a clash was coming, Abu Nidal persuaded the leaders of the PLO to send him to Iraq. In Iraq, he argued, he could arrange the delivery of money and arms to the PLO from the Iraqis. He could also hold the Iraqis to a promise they had made to intervene directly, in case of fighting, by using Iraqi forces stationed in Jordan to fight for the Palestinians.

The situation in Jordan worsened when a Palestinian

Sabri Khalil al-Banna—known to the world as Abu Nidal

group hijacked three airliners and had them land in Jordan. The hijackings embarrassed King Hussein, and in September 1970, open warfare broke out. Hussein sent units of the Jordanian army into the streets of Amman and into the Palestinian camps. After several days of fighting, the Jordanians drove the PLO out of Amman and eventually out of the kingdom.

Iraq, meanwhile, had done nothing to help—the Iraqi forces stationed in Jordan did not move. Worse, the PLO's own representative—Abu Nidal—began to attack Fatah and the PLO leadership publicly over a Baghdad radio station. In harsh words, he accused

Arafat and other PLO leaders of cowardice and treachery.

In the short period of time he had been in Baghdad, Abu Nidal had become an agent of the Iraqi government. Many in the PLO suspected that he had been recruited in Khartoum by the Iraqis. Although he was still an official PLO representative, he had formed his own faction to oppose Yasir Arafat.

Like Syria, Iraq was run by a Ba'athist government that took a hard line toward Israel. The leaders of Iraq saw in Abu Nidal a convenient agent for action against their enemies. The government provided him with money and arms and allowed him to set up training camps in northern Iraq. The Iraqis also cooperated

Jordanian soldiers and an armored car advance down a street in the capital, Amman, as they battle Palestinian guerrillas.

with actions Abu Nidal carried out with the guerrillas trained at these camps.

Abu Nidal had paid close attention to terrorist acts of the late 1960s and early 1970s. He opposed the hit-and-run raids carried out by the PLO into Israel. These raids gained little notice outside the Middle East and were causing heavy losses among Palestinian fighters. Instead of this guerrilla warfare, he preferred the careful planning that went into laying bombs and assassinating prominent people. He also sought to gain publicity by targeting western Europe, where terrorist acts attracted more coverage by television and newspapers.

Abu Nidal planned his first operation for September 1973. A conference of several nations was taking place in Algeria. Representatives from Kuwait, Saudi Arabia, the PLO, and the United Nations were meeting to decide on a common policy toward Israel. The leaders of Iraq, which had been left out of the conference, sought to disrupt the meeting with an act of terrorism. To oblige his hosts, Abu Nidal planned the seizure of the Saudi embassy in Paris.

On September 5, five of Abu Nidal's men burst into the embassy. They took 13 hostages out of the building and put them on a plane to Kuwait. They ordered the plane's pilot to fly to Riyadh, then back to Kuwait. Although the hijackers demanded the release of Abu Dawud, a Fatah leader imprisoned in Jordan, their real mission was to disrupt the Algiers conference. They were successful on both counts. The Jordanian king released Abu Dawud, and the action became a great embarrassment for Yasir Arafat and the PLO, who came under harsh criticism for the hijacking.

When several PLO leaders confronted Abu Nidal in Baghdad, Iraqi leaders came to his defense, claiming that Iraq had, in fact, directed the operation. The PLO leadership realized that they had lost all hope of bringing Abu Nidal back within their ranks. With the support of Iraq, Abu Nidal had become one of Fatah's most dangerous enemies. In July 1974, a plot to murder a Fatah official was uncovered in Damascus, Syria. When a Fatah investigation found evidence that Abu Nidal was behind the plot, the organization sentenced Abu Nidal to death.

Abu Nidal, however, was living safely and openly in Iraq. The Iraqi regime had turned over to him all of Fatah's property in Baghdad and had also given him several million dollars with which to build his organization. With his growing wealth and reputation, Abu Nidal attracted scores of Fatah fighters to his camps.

Like many members of the PLO, Abu Nidal believed that terrorism was the most effective weapon the Palestinians could use. In the early 1970s, he set up a military committee to plan terrorist operations in Europe and the Middle East. Members of the group smuggled weapons into Europe inside Iraqi diplomatic bags. (The bags, which are usually used for secret documents, cannot be searched by border guards.) The group also concealed weapons in cars that Iraqi ships

Amid many protests, Yasir Arafat—the hated rival of Abu Nidal—addresses the United Nations General Assembly in November 1974.

brought into European ports. When the weapons reached their destinations—usually near large cities—they were put in hiding places where Abu Nidal's men could find them and use them when necessary.

Although he was now the head of a large and self-sufficient organization, Abu Nidal was still acting at the direction of the Iraqi government. The Iraqis were seeking to become the leaders of the Arab world and the champions of the Palestinian cause. Iraq also opposed Arafat, who in the early 1970s, announced his willingness to negotiate with Israel over the future of the Palestinians. To undermine and strike at Arafat, Abu

Nidal's gunmen murdered several PLO ambassadors in western Europe.

Although they both had Ba'athist governments, Syria and Iraq were feuding over the political leadership of the Arab world. In 1976, Syria's intervention in a civil war in Lebanon earned the anger of many Arab countries. The Iraqis decided to use Abu Nidal's organization to attack Syria with a terrorist campaign. Bombs exploded at the offices of the Syrian national airlines in Kuwait and in Rome. Terrorists took 90 hostages during a raid at the Semiramis Hotel in Damascus. They also attacked the Syrian embassies in Pakistan and in Italy.

Not all of Abu Nidal's operations succeeded, however. In October 1977, one of his gunmen fired at a Syrian minister in Abu Dhabi, the capital of United Arab Emirates (UAE), a Persian Gulf nation. Although the assassin missed the Syrian, his bullets killed a UAE government official.

In 1979, when Abu Nidal suffered a heart attack, doctors rushed him to a hospital in Sweden for an operation. He appointed Naji Allush, a Lebanese, to direct the organization in his place. Allush was a harsh critic of Yasir Arafat and the PLO. But, unknown to Abu Nidal, he also sought to start his own Palestinian resistance movement with Abu Nidal's men. Abu Nidal, for his part, was trying to use Allush to build a terrorist underground in Lebanon. After moving to Baghdad, Allush tried to recruit followers to his cause. Although some of Abu Nidal's men joined Allush, most remained loyal to their leader.

After this attempted takeover of his organization, Abu Nidal began to fear for his life. He went underground and told no one—not even his close associates—of his whereabouts. To relieve his pain and stress, his doctors had prescribed a small daily dose of whiskey. Abu Nidal soon began drinking heavily, and he eventually became an alcoholic. Many believe that Abu Nidal's drinking and isolation seriously affected his judgment.

In 1981, Abu Nidal moved to Poland. He lived there for several years while posing as an ordinary Arab businessman. For some time, the Polish government did not know his true identity. To raise money, he set up profitable arms deals between eastern Europe and the Middle East.

At the same time, the Iraqi government was growing suspicious of Abu Nidal and his organization. Iraq's leader, Saddam Hussein, needed allies—including Jordan and the United Arab Emirates—in his war with Iran. Abu Nidal's terrorist attacks against these countries were becoming an embarrassment.

The Iraqis withheld passports from Abu Nidal's guerrillas and bugged rooms at the organization's offices in Baghdad. Finally, in November 1983, the Iraqi government expelled Abu Nidal from Baghdad. This turn of events proved to be only an inconvenience. Abu Nidal was willing to work for any government that was willing to provide him with safe facilities and financial support. Seeking a new patron, Abu Nidal set his eyes on Syria.

Hafez el-Assad, the Syrian leader, needed help in intimidating King Hussein of Jordan and Yasir Arafat, who were attempting to negotiate with Israel over the future of the Palestinians. The Syrian president wanted to play a greater role and press for Israel's surrender of the Golan Heights, a Syrian territory that Israel had seized during the Six-Day War in 1967. Assad demanded that Syria be included in any deal made over the occupied territories.

Abu Nidal had already moved some of his offices to Damascus by the summer of 1981. But his reputation was well known in the Middle East. Wishing to avoid an open connection with the terrorist, the Syrian government did not allow him to recruit or to train his followers except in the greatest secrecy.

Nevertheless, Assad allowed Abu Nidal to send his fighters into Lebanon, where a war between Israel, Syria, and the PLO was raging. In August 1982, Israeli forces expelled Yasir Arafat, Assad's rival, from Lebanon. In gratitude for Abu Nidal's work on their behalf, the Syrians helped him set up training camps and a headquarters in Lebanon.

A divided country with a weak central government, Lebanon made an excellent location for Abu Nidal's organization. Rival militia leaders with their own private armies held authority over the countryside and over the neighborhoods of Beirut, the Lebanese capital. Abu

*Masked fighters loyal to Abu Nidal man a barricade in
southern Lebanon.*

Nidal was able to build new bases, training camps, and
communication centers in southern Lebanon.

From 1983 until 1985, with the cooperation and
guidance of the Syrian government, Abu Nidal under-
took a campaign of terror against Jordan. His agents
attacked Jordanian ambassadors in Europe and Asia,
bombed Jordanian hotels, and hijacked Jordanian
planes.

The Jordanians knew why these attacks were occurring. In many cases, Abu Nidal directly claimed responsibility from his office in Damascus. In revenge,
Jordanian agents bombed the offices of Syrian Airlines
in Rome. Jordan also set off deadly car bombs in the
streets of Damascus.

In 1985, after nearly two years of violence and destruction, King Hussein called for a cease-fire with Assad. Hussein announced that, according to Assad's wishes, he would no longer attempt to negotiate directly with Israel. As a result, Syria pressured Abu Nidal to cease his terrorist campaign.

By this time, however, Abu Nidal was no longer dependent on the Syrians for shelter or for financial support. He controlled bases in Syria and Lebanon and was making a fortune by dealing weapons from eastern Europe. He also made millions by simply blackmailing Arab leaders with threats of bombing and murder. One of his victims was Sheikh Zayid, the ruler of the United Arab Emirates.

At first, Zayid refused to answer Abu Nidal's threats. In September 1983, however, a plane flying from Pakistan to the United Arab Emirates exploded in midair, killing all the passengers and crew. It had been carrying a suitcase bomb designed in one of Abu Nidal's camps. In February 1984, an ambassador from the UAE was murdered in Paris. Soon afterward, Sheikh Zayid agreed to cooperate with Abu Nidal's demands.

The Syrian government was keeping Abu Nidal at a distance by not allowing him to recruit openly in Syria and by not directly providing money. Other nations were demanding that Assad end his support. In 1987, Syria formally expelled Abu Nidal. But he had already found a new sponsor in the North African nation of Libya.

Colonel Muammar Qaddafi had come to power by overthrowing the Libyan king in 1969. He supported revolutionary groups in Europe, Africa, and the Middle East. He despised other Arab regimes—especially Egypt—as well as the PLO and Arafat. He held absolute power in Libya, where opposition to Qaddafi's government meant prison or death. Nevertheless, many Libyan opposition groups were operating in the capitals of western Europe, where Libyan students and exiles openly denounced Qaddafi. To silence his opponents, Qaddafi enlisted Abu Nidal's help.

Qaddafi offered Abu Nidal the use of the Libyan intelligence services, as well as a large training camp in the Libyan desert. Worried for his own safety, Abu Nidal sought more protection than he could find in either Syria or Lebanon. In return for Qaddafi's support, he helped the Libyan leader obtain arms and murder his opponents in Europe.

The year 1985 was a busy one for Abu Nidal's organization. His men carried out the bombing of the United States embassy in Egypt and the hijacking of an Egyptian plane to the island of Malta. The bloody attacks at airports in Rome and Vienna followed in December. When the United States bombed Libya in April 1986, Abu Nidal responded with a massacre at a synagogue in Istanbul, Turkey.

In Lebanon, however, guerrillas from the PLO and from the Abu Nidal organization often found themselves fighting on the same side. The People's Army, a

Libya's leader Muammar Qaddafi has armed, trained, and funded international terrorism for more than two decades.

militia of Abu Nidal's men, had become one of the largest private armies in the country. But their leader was hundreds of miles away in a remote Libyan camp. Distrusting the leaders of the People's Army and fearing that many of his aides were turning against him, Abu Nidal ordered the execution of many of his men in southern Lebanon. Hundreds were shot and then buried in unmarked graves. As a result of this bloodshed, many of Abu Nidal's followers abandoned him in the late 1980s.

By the early 1990s, Abu Nidal's organization was split in two, with rival factions operating in Libya and in

Lebanon. In the early morning hours of June 8, 1992, a member of the PLO, Atef Bseiso, was shot and killed in front of a Paris hotel. Two gunmen fled from the hotel and evaded capture. A few days later, two phone calls were made to newspapers in Beirut. One caller denied any involvement in the murder; the other claimed responsibility for Bseiso's death. Both calls were made in the name of Abu Nidal.

In Libya, Abu Nidal still leads a large organization of loyal aides and soldiers. He lives well under Qaddafi's protection. He has profited handsomely from murder and blackmail, while claiming to fight for the Palestinians. But with the support of Iraq and now Libya, his most frequent targets have been members of the PLO—the organization that has been, for many years, the strongest voice for the Palestinian cause. Instead of a Palestinian nationalist, Abu Nidal has become a Middle Eastern gangster who has mastered the methods of terror.

German terrorist leader Ulrike Meinhof in police custody after her arrest in June 1975

6

The Baader-Meinhof Gang

*T*errorism occurs in rich as well as in poor societies. Since the French Revolution, many of those who have committed acts of political violence have been from the middle class. Others were students who rejected the customs and morals of their parents' generation. This was true in West Germany during the 1960s and 1970s, a time when students throughout western Europe found much in their societies to criticize.

Germany—now one of the richest nations in the world—was defeated and later divided at the end of World War II in 1945. After occupying the country, the forces of the United States, Great Britain, France, and the Soviet Union set up four zones of occupation. In the east, the Soviet government installed a Communist regime, in which the state owned all land, homes, and businesses. The Soviets strictly controlled the lives of the people of East Germany and did not allow them to travel to West Germany.

The pre-war German capital of Berlin, which lay in East Germany, was also divided into four zones. The western half of the city was controlled by the United States, Britain, and France; the Soviet Union controlled the eastern part. In the early 1960s, to prevent their people from fleeing communism, the Soviet-backed East German government built a massive wall of concrete and barbed wire around West Berlin. Many East Germans who attempted to climb the wall and escape were shot.

Despite the barrier that surrounded it, West Berlin was a lively city, full of writers, artists, and students. West Berliners shopped at large department stores and gathered at busy restaurants and cafes. The city had churches, libraries, parks, and a famous zoo. Thousands of West Germans born during or after the war enrolled in West Berlin's prestigious universities.

During the 1960s, many of these students abandoned their classrooms to march in the streets. They demanded an end to the Vietnam War and the reform of university administrations. Many who were bored with material goods mocked West Berlin's prosperous middle class. Demonstrators expressed their opposition by throwing eggs, paint, and firecrackers in the streets and in university lecture halls.

The students organized small groups to press their

demands for change. Several "left-wing" West German magazines that openly favored the Communist governments of eastern Europe supported the students in their demands. To attain a Communist society like that of the Soviet Union and East Germany, the leftist students—and a few journalists—called for the violent overthrow of non-Communist governments.

One man who joined the students in West Berlin was Bernd Andreas Baader. Born in Munich in 1943, Baader had lost his father during World War II and had been raised by his mother and his aunt. After failing high school, he moved to West Berlin. There Baader landed in trouble with the police, who arrested him several times for traffic violations and for stealing cars. Baader's reputation as an outlaw gained him many friends among students in West Berlin.

In the mid-1960s, Baader met Gudrun Ensslin, the daughter of a West German pastor. Ensslin's parents had raised her to oppose all forms of capitalism—the economic system of private property and free markets that was turning West Germany into a rich nation. While a student in West Berlin, Ensslin declared at meetings and at street protests that she was committed to remaking German society by whatever means necessary.

As the student protests grew larger, they grew more violent. The shooting death of a student protestor on June 2, 1967, shocked Gudrun Ensslin. She announced at meetings that the government and the police had

Andreas Baader and Gudrun Ensslin

declared war on the students. With help from Andreas
Baader and two friends, she then took her protest
beyond words. On April 2, 1968, the four planted
gasoline bombs at Kaufhof and at Schneider, two large
and popular department stores in Frankfurt, West
Germany. The stores burned for hours while passersby
and students watched from the street.

The young arsonists made the mistake of leaving
evidence in their homes and at the scene of the crime.
The police quickly found a list of explosive chemicals as
well as equipment the students had used to make time
bombs. Two days after the bombing, the police arrested all four. At her trial, Gudrun Ensslin claimed that

she had "lit a torch for Vietnam." German newspapers carried daily accounts of the trial, and one of Germany's most celebrated lawyers, Horst Mahler, volunteered to defend the group. Nevertheless, the court found Baader and Ensslin guilty and sentenced them each to serve three-year prison terms in a West Berlin jail.

The case was a sensation in West Germany. Until the Frankfurt fires, Germans had rarely seen political violence—only the throwing of eggs and paint. Newspapers and magazines ran long stories condemning the bombing, which seemed a frightening echo of the bloody terrorism that was common in the Middle East and South America. To many journalists, however, Baader and Ensslin were political prisoners—heroes who were fighting for a good cause. Instead of merely writing or talking about revolution, these students were backing up their talk with action.

One of these sympathetic journalists was Ulrike Meinhof, an editor of a leftist magazine called *Konkret*. A celebrity in West Germany, Meinhof created plays for radio and appeared regularly on television talk shows. Her columns in *Konkret*, which often condemned the West German government, were read by students and quoted by Germany's most important newspapers.

The firebombing in Frankfurt fascinated Meinhof. She attended the trial and visited the prisoners several times in their cells. Her columns in *Konkret* expressed sympathy and support for Ensslin and Baader. At the same time, Meinhof was growing unhappy with her professional success. Although she earned enough money, the opinions she expressed on television and in the magazine seemed to have no impact on events or on the government. After the trial, she moved to West Berlin.

In the autumn, after a court rejected an appeal of their sentences, Ensslin and Baader fled Germany. They traveled to France, Switzerland, Italy, and finally back to West Berlin. There they gained shelter at Ulrike Meinhof's apartment. Andreas Baader, who could not stand to remain in hiding for long, was quickly caught by the police and returned to jail.

By now a committed member of the underground, Meinhof made arrangements for Baader's escape from prison. With this single act, her life as a writer and television celebrity came to an end. She became instead one of Germany's most wanted criminals.

The plan to free Baader was simple. Horst Mahler, Baader's lawyer, created a fake letter in the name of a German publishing company. The letter, addressed to the prison authorities, stated that the company had hired Baader to write a book. But the prisoner would need to do research in the library of the German Institute for Social Questions, located in the Berlin neighborhood of Dahlen. After receiving Mahler's letter, the prison warden agreed to allow Baader to work in the library while under guard.

Meanwhile, Meinhof and several friends arranged to buy guns on the black market. On the morning of May 14, 1970, they arrived at the library in Dahlen carrying their weapons in paper bags. The prison van transporting Baader arrived soon afterward. Escorted by two guards, the prisoner entered the front hall of the building, walked through a door leading to the main room, and sat down at a desk near a window.

Within minutes, two women and a man entered the building, making a noisy disturbance. When the librarian went into the hall to investigate, he was shot. Meinhof disarmed Baader's prison guards and held them at bay. Baader and Meinhof then climbed out of the library's window and ran to a waiting car.

A few weeks later, a letter addressed to the German Press Agency announced the formation of the Red Army Faction (RAF). Germany's newspapers and magazines knew that the RAF included Andreas Baader and Ulrike Meinhof—the fugitives who had escaped through the windows of the Dahlen library. To the public, the group became known as the Baader-Meinhof Gang.

Baader, Meinhof, Ensslin, and Horst Mahler went underground in Berlin. A huge manhunt took place in the city. Thousands of police searched cars, homes, and public places. They also kept a close watch on train stations, roads, and the Berlin airport. Unable to leave West Berlin by plane, car, or train, the gang evaded the search by slipping across the Berlin Wall into

East Germany. From there, the gang flew on an East German airplane to Beirut, Lebanon.

In the late 1960s, several Palestinian terrorist organizations had moved into refugee camps near the Lebanese-Israeli border. One of these was the Popular Front for the Liberation of Palestine (PFLP). The PFLP trained its guerrillas in the camps and staged raids across the border into Israel. In 1968, the PFLP opened the camps to members of the European underground, many of whom supported Palestinian claims to Israel as their homeland. The Europeans came for several months of training in the use of arms and explosives. The PFLP then recruited them for terrorist missions in Europe.

After their arrival in the early summer of 1970, the German fugitives quickly found that life in the refugee camps was not to their taste. The training was physically demanding, and the Germans did not get along with the PFLP guerrillas. The Palestinians looked upon their guests as criminals and gangsters and viewed Andreas Baader as a coward. In August 1970, the PFLP asked the Germans to leave Lebanon.

Mahler, Baader, Ensslin, and Meinhof returned to Germany and recruited 20 new members to their Red Army Faction. Horst Mahler, who had become the group's leader, realized that large amounts of money would be needed to survive underground. To acquire the cash as well as the skills necessary in terrorist situations, Mahler planned a series of bank robberies. The gang hit three West Berlin banks on September 29, 1970.

Helped by an anonymous tip, the police arrested Mahler on October 8. Taking over as leader, Andreas Baader moved the RAF to West Germany. Two more bank robberies occurred in Kassel, West Germany, in January 1971. The group also broke into city offices to steal official papers, blank passports, and government stamps and seals. With this material, they made false passports and identity cards.

The stolen money enabled the RAF to acquire weapons and explosives through a terrorist network that linked Europe and the Middle East. George Habash, the leader of the PFLP, was using Europeans to bring the Israeli-Palestinian conflict to the nations of the West. The PFLP shipped submachine guns, plastic explosives, and ammunition through eastern Europe to the RAF and to other groups in France and Italy.

In the spring of 1972, after the robberies in West Germany, the RAF decided to attack U.S. military forces stationed there. On May 24, the group exploded pipe bombs outside the Campbell Barracks at U.S. Army headquarters in Heidelberg. Hidden in two parked cars, the 50-pound bombs killed two men—an officer and a civilian—and injured several others. Another bomb exploded at the army's officers' club in Frankfurt.

The violence shocked West Germany. Baader and Meinhof announced that their actions were meant to

Lawyer-turned-criminal Horst Mahler appears in a West German courtroom with his attorney.

ignite a class war. By setting off bombs and killing people—at well-defended military bases—they sought to create a state of panic. A massive uprising of the country's farmers and workers would end, they hoped, with the overthrow of the government.

The plan failed. Instead of bringing down the government, the RAF's terrorism caused a crackdown. Frightened by the violence, the West German legislature passed tough new laws with little opposition from the press or the public. Before being hired, government employees would now be required to pass loyalty tests. Other laws restricted the stories and opinions that newspapers and magazines could print. In addition, any lawyer suspected of aiding or sympathizing with terrorists could be banned from appearing in court.

The police had more success than the legislature in stopping the RAF. They captured the gang's leaders in 1972, soon after the bombings. On June 1, in Frankfurt, an antiterrorist unit ambushed and captured Andreas Baader in a garage used for assembling bombs. One week later, the police arrested Gudrun Ensslin in a Hamburg shop. A clerk had noticed a pistol in her coat and had contacted the police. On June 15, a friend with whom she had been staying turned in Ulrike Meinhof.

The RAF leaders remained in jail for several years as the government prepared to put them on trial. As their lawyers used tactics to delay and disrupt the trial, the gang members planned escapes. Prison guards eventually discovered all these schemes. To secure their prisoners, the government built special cells for them at Stammheim Prison, near Stuttgart. They kept the prisoners under constant surveillance. The walls of their cells were painted white, and their cell lights burned 24 hours a day.

The prison conditions took their toll. On May 9, 1976, after several months of solitary confinement, Ulrike Meinhof committed suicide by hanging herself from the bars of her jail cell. In April 1977, the courts sentenced Andreas Baader and Gudrun Ensslin to life terms.

Although the RAF's leaders were now out of circulation, other members of the group were still operating in West Germany. On the afternoon of September 5, 1977, Hans Martin Schleyer, a wealthy German businessman, was riding home from work in a chauffered car. Several bodyguards riding in a car behind him provided escort. When a baby carriage suddenly appeared in the middle of the road, Schleyer's driver stopped. The car in the rear then smashed into Schleyer's car.

Immediately, a van appeared. Several men ran from the van to the second car, firing on and killing the bodyguards. They turned to Schleyer's car, shot the driver, pulled the wealthy businessman from the car, and drove away in the van.

The kidnappers sent a photo of their victim as well as a note demanding the immediate release of the RAF leaders, who were also to be provided with money. Otherwise, the note said, Schleyer would be killed. Several deadlines passed, but the German government refused to meet these demands.

On October 13, 1977, another group of terrorists hijacked a flight of Lufthansa, the German national airline. The hijackers demanded the release of the Red Army Faction leaders. After the plane landed in South Yemen—a small country on the Arabian peninsula—the hijackers murdered the pilot. They then ordered the copilot to fly the plane to Mogadishu, the capital of Somalia.

Unknown to the hijackers, an antiterrorist unit had followed them from Germany. The second plane carried trained commandos and a full load of arms and explosives. At Mogadishu, the second plane landed behind the hijacked Lufthansa flight. Almost immediately, the commandos stormed the plane, killing three of the hijackers. The passengers escaped unhurt from the plane, and the commandos captured the remaining terrorist.

The government seemed to have scored a victory. But the next morning, Andreas Baader was found dead in his cell. He had been shot. Gang member Gudrun Ensslin was found hanging from the iron bars of her window. Although many suspected the RAF leaders had been murdered, the doctor who performed an autopsy on the bodies declared their deaths to be suicide. Soon after the authorities discovered Baader's body, Schleyer's kidnappers carried out their threat and murdered him.

The deaths of Baader, Meinhof, and Ensslin did not end terrorist acts within Germany. The remaining members of the RAF continued to target military installations. The gang bombed U.S. bases in 1981 and 1982 and carried out several assassinations. On May 11, 1981, they shot and killed Heinz Karry, a government official who had offered rewards for the capture of Baader-Meinhof members.

Heinz Herbert Karry, economics minister from the West German state of Hesse, paid with his life for standing up to the Baader-Meinhof Gang.

By the early 1980s, however, the RAF was down to a few dozen members. The German government was offering leniency to terrorists who surrendered. Several of the founders of the RAF took advantage of this offer and turned themselves in. Many of them served no time in prison.

During the 1980s, with terrorist violence increasing around the world, Europe turned more of its resources to capturing the members of terrorist groups that had sprung up in Germany, Italy, and France. By the early 1990s, most political violence in Europe no longer represented the actions of student terrorists. Instead, nationalist conflicts in Northern Ireland and in the Basque region of Spain were the source of most political violence. The generation of students now attending European universities, where many of the terrorist groups of the 1970s began, has no taste for bank robberies, kidnapping, and bombing. With fewer recruits and most of its members dead or in prison, the RAF has disappeared from the scene.

To prove that their prisoner, the kidnapped Italian ex-premier Aldo Moro, was still alive, the Red Brigades released this photograph of him holding the previous day's newspaper.

110

7

The Red Brigades

*I*taly, an ally of Germany during World War II, recovered slowly from the war. The Italian government was split into competing factions—Christian Democrats, Republicans, Socialists—and was unstable and ineffective. Unemployment and inflation were high. Organized crime flourished. Many Italians were convinced that an entirely new form of government was needed. Others believed that there was only one way to bring about change—violence.

The economic problems turned many Italians to communism. By the 1970s, the Communist party of Italy had won control of many city councils, especially in the northern half of the country. Nearly two million Italians, many of them factory workers, were members of the party. Enrico Berlinguer, Italy's Communist leader, vowed that his party respected democracy and would

111

take no orders from the communist leaders of the Soviet Union. Many Italian politicians and voters, however, didn't believe him.

One man who was willing to cooperate with the Communists was Aldo Moro, the leader of the Christian Democratic party. Moro was a popular leader from Bari, a town in southern Italy. By the late 1970s, the Italians had elected him prime minister of Italy five times. In 1978, he was once again preparing to assume this office. To avoid a divided government, he was planning to form a coalition of five parties to rule the country. For the first time, this ruling coalition would include the Communist party.

Many of Moro's allies strongly opposed Communist participation. The United States and the NATO organization, to which Italy belonged, were armed and prepared for war with the Communist nations of eastern Europe. As a result, the U.S. and many of its allies in western Europe did not want to see Communist politicians accepted into the highest levels of the Italian government.

An organization known as the *Brigate Rosse*—the Red Brigades—also opposed Moro's coalition. Members of the Red Brigades were former Communists who refused to participate in the government. They saw no hope in cooperating with Moro, with the Christian Democrats, or with any other political group in Italy. Instead, they took their opposition one step further with the use of terror.

The Red Brigades were founded in 1970 by two students, Renato Curcio and Margherita Cagol. Both studied sociology. Curcio was planning to become a chemist, Cagol an accountant. They were practicing Roman Catholics and were married after graduating from the University of Trent.

Even though they both came from the middle class, Curcio and Cagol fervently believed in the communist slogan of "all power to the workers." Like many Italian students, they believed workers and farmers should share ownership of the country's factories and farms. Social classes should be abolished, and government power given only to Communist leaders. This message had great appeal in Italy, where a divided and unstable democratic government seemed unable to solve the country's problems.

After becoming members of the Communist party, Curcio and Cagol joined the labor movement in northern Italy. They soon adopted illegal methods of carrying out the workers' struggle. With the help of workers sympathetic to their cause, they sabotaged factories and burned the cars of spies who worked for factory owners. At many demonstrations, they prompted the workers to violence against the police.

As their faces became more familiar to the Italian police, Cagol and Curcio went underground to continue their fight. Eventually, both left the Communist party to begin the Red Brigades. A small group of committed workers and students joined them.

Curcio divided the group into "columns" that were based in major Italian cities: Genoa, Turin, Milan, and Rome. These columns were made up of cells, each of which included up to six members (called *brigatistas*). Cell commanders reported to column commanders, who controlled all of the cells in a certain city. The members of one cell, however, did not know the identities of the members of other cells. In this way, captured brigatistas were unable to reveal information under interrogation about different Red Brigade columns.

In the early 1970s, the group began a bombing campaign. It set off explosives in factories in Milan and Genoa in northern Italy. In addition, the Red Brigades raised money from bank robberies and from the kidnapping of wealthy businessmen for ransom.

One of the group's first victims was Ettore Amerio, a director of personnel for Fiat, the huge Italian auto company. In 1973, after Fiat fired 250 Communist activists at one of its plants, the Red Brigades kidnapped Amerio. The group presented a simple demand to the company: no more firings. In response, Fiat promised not to lay off any more workers, and the Red Brigades quickly released Amerio.

The Red Brigades also targeted government officials. Mario Sossi, a public prosecutor from Genoa, was an outspoken enemy of leftist activists and of the Red Brigades. In the spring of 1974, the group kidnapped Sossi, held him in a small cell, and demanded the release of eight brigatistas from prison. Although a Genoa court decided to release the prisoners, the city's government blocked their release at the last minute. The Red Brigades freed Sossi anyway. The leaders felt that by living up to their part of the bargain, they had made an important point about the corruption and dishonesty of the Italian government.

By 1975, the Red Brigades had recruited about 500 brigatistas. The group had stolen enough money to pay each member several hundred dollars a month. Using these fighters as its core, the Red Brigades planned to disrupt Italian society. With bombings, assassinations,

Although a kidnapping victim of the Red Brigades, Mario Sossi could easily have suffered a worse fate at their hands.

115

and kidnappings, they hoped to rouse Italy's workers to violence that would end in revolution. The organization enjoyed the support of many journalists and of university students and professors.

In 1975, the Red Brigades began using more violent methods. The group targeted several businessmen and members of the Christian Democratic party to be "kneecapped"—shot in the legs and crippled. Because bombings and street violence resulted in deaths and injuries, the group began losing many of its sympathizers among Italy's middle class.

The growing number of members also made the group's leaders easier to trace when the police captured and questioned brigatistas. In June 1975, Margherita Cagol was followed to a farmhouse and killed in a shoot-out. In January 1976, police traced Curcio to an apartment in Milan. After a 20-minute gun battle, Curcio surrendered. The government announced that he would be put on trial.

The Red Brigades survived the loss of its founders. The members of the group had no intention of allowing a state trial of Curcio. It threatened lawyers, witnesses, and judges, and carried out several assassinations.

In the winter of 1978, as Curcio waited in a Turin jail for his trial, the new leaders of the Red Brigades began planning to free their leader. Since Curcio's prison was well guarded, the Red Brigades laid plans to take an important hostage. This action, they thought, would force the government into a prisoner exchange.

Former university students Renato Curcio (above) and Margherita Cagol strongly condemned their middle-class upringing and sought through violence to create a classless society. Toward this goal, the couple founded the Red Brigades. Both Curcio and Cagol would ultimately pay dearly for the group's terrorist activities.

117

The Red Brigades decided to strike at the top—at Aldo Moro.

On March 16, accompanied by a chauffeur and a bodyguard, Moro left his home in a wealthy neighborhood of Rome. This was the day that the legislature would vote on his new governing coalition. An Alfa Romeo car that carried four bodyguards—and an arsenal of weapons in its locked trunk—followed him. At a small intersection only a few hundred yards from Moro's home, a small, white Fiat station wagon pulled in front of his car and slammed to a stop.

After the Alfa Romeo carrying his bodyguards hit the rear of his own car, Moro's driver hesitated. He was unable to move forward or backward. A man and a woman jumped from the white Fiat and walked over to Moro's car. Without hesitating, they pulled guns from their coats and shot the driver and a bodyguard to death.

Immediately, four men who had been standing on the sidewalk walked over to the Alfa Romeo. They raked the four bodyguards with a deadly hail of bullets. The terrorists pulled Moro from his car and shoved him into a nearby van. Two days later, the Red Brigades declared that Moro was in captivity and would be put on trial.

The government had an important decision to make. Although one of Italy's most powerful men was now a hostage, Italy's leaders did not want to be seen negotiating with terrorists. In addition, the members of Italy's

Communist party were determined to stay in the ruling coalition that Moro had arranged. If the public believed that the Communists were sympathetic to the Red Brigades, the coalition would collapse. For this reason, the Communist leaders took a hard line and opposed any negotiation with the kidnappers.

Although Moro sent several open letters asking the government to negotiate, Italy's newspapers—which were controlled by the country's various political parties—declared that the letters could not possibly be sincere. Journalists speculated that the terrorists were using drugs or hypnosis to force Moro to write the letters.

Giulio Andreotti, the prime minister, announced that his government would not negotiate under any circumstances. The trial of Renato Curcio would proceed as planned. The government began a massive search and asked the press to censor items involving Moro's kidnapping. The police searched or questioned more than 10 million Italians—more than 20 percent of the population.

In letters to his family, delivered by Red Brigade couriers, Moro called for members of the Christian Democrats to oppose Andreotti's stand. Moro suggested that his captors would accept a simple, one-for-one prisoner exchange. On May 5, the Red Brigades publicly announced that Moro's trial was over. He, and the Italian government, had been found guilty. Moro would be executed. To emphasize its determination, the group kneecapped a Christian Democrat politician in Rome and a Fiat executive in Turin.

Andreotti was strongly supported in his position by other members of the Italian government and by the United States. Although the Socialists and some members of the Christian Democrats were asking the government to negotiate for Moro, Andreotti was unbending. On May 6, Moro's family and members of the Socialist party proposed the release of a single brigatista, who was terminally ill, from jail.

On May 9, while the debate continued within the government, Moro's body was found in the trunk of a car in Rome. He had been shot several times in the chest at close range. The coalition government fell through. In the next month, the Italian courts sentenced Renato Curcio to 15 years in prison.

The killings and maimings in Italian cities continued, at times reaching such frequency that the government appeared quite helpless. Public places—airports, post offices, and train stations—were under constant armed guard. By 1980, about 100 different terrorist groups—many of them connected in some way with the Red Brigades—were operating in Italy.

Italian terrorism was occurring on both sides of the political spectrum. In 1980, a right-wing group planted a bomb in the central train station of Bologna, a city known for its pro-Communist workers and students. The bomb exploded at a busy hour, killing 80 people and injuring hundreds.

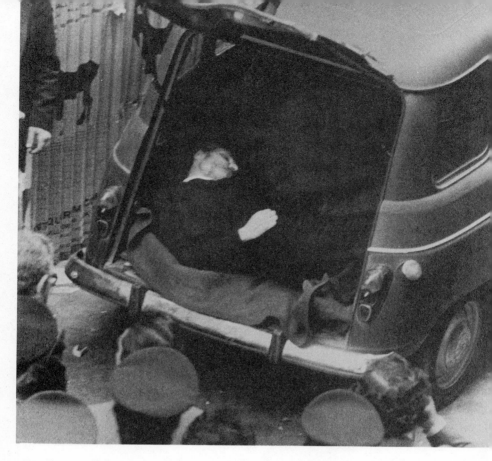

The body of Aldo Moro, discovered in a car parked on a Rome street

The weak Italian government did not set a clear policy to fight terrorism. In addition, the many police agencies operating within Italy were badly coordinated. Information held by the national police force—known as the *carabinieri*—was not shared with city police forces. The carabinieri and the city police also lacked antiterrorist training.

In the early 1980s, the government finally had some success with a program that offered leniency to terrorists who surrendered. Several hundred terrorists took

Within a few years of the 1981 capture of Mario Moretti, here behind bars, the Red Brigades had vanished from the political scene.

advantage of the offer and became *penitenti*—"penitents." In 1981, the police caught Mario Moretti, a Red Brigades leader from Milan, and announced that they had caught the leader and organizer of the Moro kidnapping. Many believed that with Moretti's arrest the police had broken the Red Brigades.

In December, however, four terrorists disguised as plumbers kidnapped U.S. Brigadier General James L. Dozier from his apartment in Verona, where he worked as an officer at NATO headquarters. The kidnappers tied up Dozier's wife and carried the general out of his apartment building in a trunk.

Within a few weeks, the police traced Dozier's captors to an apartment in Padua, in northern Italy. On January 26, 1982, an antiterrorist squad burst into the apartment. The team had brought bulldozers into the street outside the apartment to drown out noise. They found Dozier inside a large tent. They also discovered detailed files, giving the names and addresses of hundreds of kidnapping targets. The courts tried and sentenced the kidnappers in March 1982.

The government passed a new law that offered leniency to *brigatistas* already in prison. More than 300 members of the Red Brigades were brought into custody after the Dozier kidnapping. But one of these, Roberto Peci, was caught, tortured, and murdered by members of the Red Brigades. After Peci's death, fewer informants came forth as *penitenti*. The government called off its leniency program in 1983.

As more members of the Red Brigades surrendered or left the organization, political terrorism began dying out in Italy in the mid-1980s. Nevertheless, the government had other serious problems to confront. One of the worst of these was organized crime. A criminal network known as the Mafia has succeeded in intimidating the country's judges and lawyers through bombings and assassination. Several of the country's leading prosecutors have lost their lives. Although it has succeeded in curbing terrorism, the Italian government is now facing a more serious threat from organized crime.

A Hezbollah fighter stands in southern Lebanon before pictures of his spiritual leader, the Ayatollah Ruhollah Khomeini.

8

Hezbollah

The truck sped down Beirut's airport road, quickly arriving outside the heavily guarded walls of its target. The driver ignored the shouted orders to stop and crashed the truck through a flimsy wooden barricade. In front of him stood a long, concrete building. The driver rammed the front of the building, came to a stop, and pressed a switch in the cab. Twenty thousand pounds of explosives detonated a few feet behind him.

In an instant, tons of broken concrete and twisted steel had buried more than 200 U.S. Marines. The truck and its driver were blown to pieces. Within a few weeks, the United States would remove its forces from the war-torn nation of Lebanon. In the name of the Ayatollah Khomeini and Hezbollah, one man's suicide had forced the world's most powerful nation into a humiliating retreat.

In the late 1970s, Khomeini, an Islamic clergyman from the Middle Eastern nation of Iran, lived in exile. The government of Iran, under the rule of Shah Reza Pahlavi, had forced Khomeini to leave his homeland. From Iraq and from France, Khomeini used an inexpensive tape recorder to record his fiery, revolutionary sermons. His followers smuggled the tapes into Iran, where they were copied and sold by the thousands.

The Shi'ite Muslims of Iran revered Khomeini as their spiritual leader. (The Shi'ites are an Islamic sect with members in many Middle Eastern countries, including Iraq, a nation west of Iran, and Lebanon.) In Iran, the Shi'ites form a majority of the population. Khomeini and his Shi'ite followers believed in government based strictly on the laws of Islam. Through his recorded sermons, Khomeini called on Iranians to overthrow the shah and establish an Islamic government.

The shah of Iran employed a modern army and a large network of secret police to control his country. He made billions from the sale of Iran's oil and also had the support of the United States. But anger towards his harsh regime erupted in a violent rebellion in 1978. The Revolutionary Guards, a militia loyal to Khomeini, attacked government forces with grenades, machine guns, and homemade bombs.

Unable to put down the rebellion, the shah fled Iran in 1979. The Ayatollah Khomeini soon made a triumphant return, and quickly carried out his promise to replace the shah with an Islamic government. Religious law, as interpreted by Khomeini, became the law of the land. The Revolutionary Guards became Khomeini's police force, using violence to enforce the new Islamic code. The revolutionary government executed thousands of Iranians who had supported the shah.

Iran's revolution stunned leaders throughout the Middle East. The Shi'ite Muslims in Lebanon also took notice. But within Lebanon, the Shi'ites made up only one of many religious and ethnic groups that were fighting for political power. Christians controlled northern Lebanon; Muslims, the south. The army of Syria, a neighboring country, occupied the Bekaa Valley in central Lebanon. Since 1975, Christians, Muslims, and Syrians had been fighting in much of Lebanon.

The civil war in Lebanon was a disaster for the Shi'ites. Thousands were killed, and many more lost their homes. The Shi'ites in southern Lebanon had also endured deadly bombing raids from Israel, which lay across the border to the south. The Shi'ite militia, known as Amal, was losing ground in the war. Many Shi'ites who felt betrayed by Amal's leaders looked to Khomeini's Islamic revolution to help their cause.

The situation in Lebanon had grown even more chaotic with the arrival of the Palestine Liberation Organization (PLO). In the 1970s, many PLO fighters moved into southern Lebanon. Refugee camps for Palestinian civilians were taken over by the PLO. From these camps, PLO guerrillas staged raids on northern Israel. Israel retaliated with bombardments that destroyed Shi'ite villages and farms. With Amal unable to control the region, the Shi'ites were trapped in the conflict between Israel and the Palestinians.

On June 6, 1982, the Israeli army invaded southern Lebanon, overruning PLO camps and driving north as far as Beirut. At first, many Lebanese—including the Shi'ites—welcomed the chance to drive out the Palestinians, who were in control of much of southern Lebanon. Gradually, however, the Lebanese Shi'ites turned against the Israelis. In mosques and village squares throughout southern Lebanon, Shi'ite clerics began calling for a *jihad* (holy war) against the Israeli forces. Within a few months of the Israeli invasion, the Iranian government sent Islamic clerics into Lebanon to organize Hezbollah—the Party of God.

The Ayatollah Khomeini appointed the Hezbollah leaders and supported the group with money and arms. A Lebanese Shi'ite cleric, Sheikh Mohammed Hassan Fadlallah, became a leader of the Hezbollah. Under his guidance, Hezbollah groups sprang up in towns throughout southern Lebanon and in the Shi'ite sub-urbs south of the capital of Beirut. By using Hezbollah, Khomeini hoped to defeat Israel, bring down the weak government of Lebanon, and establish a Shi'ite Muslim state in Lebanon.

Hezbollah grew quickly, gaining thousands of mem-bers from the ranks of Amal. Its Islamic program united the poor Shi'ites of Lebanon in a common cause. New members dedicated themselves to founding a new

Hezbollah guerrillas take aim at their Israeli foes in southern Lebanon.

Islamic state, free from the influence of European nations and the United States.

The Hezbollah never grew large enough to face the Israelis, the Syrians, or the PLO directly on the front lines. Instead, the group attacked its targets with bombings, kidnappings, and hijackings. In a short time, Hezbollah became the most feared terrorist organization in the Middle East.

By 1983, the Lebanese civil war had drawn in Israel and Syria and was threatening to turn the Middle East into an international battleground. To prevent this, Italy, Britain, France, and the United States sent troops into Lebanon. Sheikh Fadlallah and the leaders of Hezbollah saw this as a direct threat to their goal of establishing an Islamic state in Lebanon.

Religious leader Sheikh Mohammad Hassan Fadlallah, a follower of the Ayatollah Khomeini, helped to organize the Hezbollah in Lebanon.

To attack the multinational forces, Hezbollah invented a terrible new weapon—the suicide truck bomb. The group loaded several hundred pounds of explosives into a truck. A member of the group—someone prepared to sacrifice his or her life—would drive the truck in front of an embassy or into a military base. The driver then set off the explosives with a control switch in the truck's cab. The detonation would instantly destroy the driver, the truck, and any buildings or people standing within several hundred feet.

Sheikh Fadlallah and Hezbollah never took credit for these attacks. As a Shi'ite cleric, Fadlallah knew that Islam forbids terrorism and the killing of innocent civilians. Fadlallah also claimed to be running Hezbollah as a political, not a military, organization.

Many Islamic nations, however, have declared jihads

130

against enemies. For this reason, an organization calling itself the "Islamic Jihad" publicly claimed responsibility for terrorist acts in Lebanon. For several years, the United States and other governments tried to find out who was running the Islamic Jihad. In fact, Hezbollah and Islamic Jihad were one and the same.

Hezbollah's deadly truck bombs forced France, Italy, Britain, and the United States to withdraw their forces from Lebanon in the spring of 1984. Seeking safety, the United States also moved its embassy to a more secure building in East Beirut, the Christian section of the city. To prevent an attack, workers set up concrete barriers in front of the embassy. But these security measures failed. In September, a Hezbollah driver crashed through the barriers and set off a thunderous explosion. The truck bomb killed 23 and destroyed the front of the building.

The attacks in Lebanon prompted the government of the United States to use the CIA—the U.S. spy agency—to investigate the bombings. The CIA discovered that Sheikh Fadlallah's Hezbollah was responsible for the attacks. To strike back, the CIA hired Lebanese agents to attack Fadlallah. On March 8, 1984, a CIA agent parked a car filled with explosives in front of the sheikh's home in south Beirut. The explosion destroyed the building and killed 80 people. Sheikh Fadlallah escaped—he had been away from the building at the time.

The attack on Fadlallah's house made the Hezbollah even more determined to hit U.S. targets. In April

1984, after the U.S. attack on Fadlallah's headquarters, Hezbollah terrorists bombed a restaurant near a U.S. military base in Torrejon, Spain, killing 18 people. Most were U.S. servicemen.

In the summer of 1985, Israel withdrew its army from southern Lebanon. The invasion of 1982 and three years of occupation had accomplished little. Civil war still raged in Lebanon, and the Lebanese government had no control over most of the country. To prevent attacks across the border, the Israelis set up a narrow security zone north of the Lebanese border and hired a Lebanese Christian army to guard it. In this way, Israeli leaders hoped to protect their country from the troubles in Lebanon.

The withdrawal of Israel left southern Lebanon

Following the attempt on Fadlallah's life, residents hang anti-American banners from the blown-out apartment building.

without any single authority in control. With the PLO driven out, Amal, Hezbollah, and other militias fought openly for control of Shi'ite territory.

Although they wished to avoid a direct connection to terrorism, the Shi'ite clerics in charge of Hezbollah also sought publicity. They believed they could gain sympathy and support from abroad by making their demands through the news media. They also hoped that this strategy would lead to the release of Hezbollah prisoners held by Israel and Kuwait, an Arab nation opposed to Hezbollah's activities.

To gain media coverage, Hezbollah began to hijack commercial airliners. By taking a plane's crew and passengers hostage, Hezbollah could prolong one of its operations for days or even weeks, drawing the attention of millions of people through newspapers and television. In June 1985, Hezbollah carried out one of the longest terrorist operations in history—the hijacking of TWA Flight 847.

Flight 847 began on June 14, in Athens, Greece. The plane was scheduled to fly to Rome, Italy. But soon after takeoff, several men rose from their seats, produced guns, and ordered the plane's captain to fly to Beirut. After the plane landed, the hijackers released 19 passengers. Several more Hezbollah terrorists then boarded the plane for the next leg of the journey—a flight to Algiers, Algeria. Hezbollah made public its demands: the Israeli government must release hundreds of Hezbollah and Palestinian prisoners or the hijackers would shoot, one by one, the passengers and crew of Flight 847.

By this time, television coverage of the hijacking was bringing the operation directly into the living rooms of millions of people around the world. The publicity put enormous pressure on the Israelis, who had vowed to make no deals with Hezbollah or any other terrorist groups.

On June 15, the plane flew back to Beirut. The hijackers now sought the help of Amal, which controlled neighborhoods near the Beirut airport. To prove their threats were serious, the hijackers marched Robert Stetham, a U.S. serviceman, to the front of the plane. There they shot Stetham and threw his lifeless body onto the ground beneath the plane. Soon afterward, Nabih Berri, the leader of Amal, sent several of his militia onto the plane to negotiate.

Hezbollah intended to prolong the hijacking as long as possible. At each stop, the hijackers released a few more passengers, giving the media fresh news. After flying to Algiers once again and then returning to Beirut, the terrorists took the remaining 44 hostages off the plane and hid them in the suburbs of Beirut. Amal, Sheikh Fadlallah, and the government of Iran then began negotiations with Israel.

On June 24, Hezbollah brought the remaining hostages out of their hiding places in Beirut, drove them to Damascus, Syria, and then flew them to Frankfurt, Germany. In the meantime, Israel had agreed to release

Leader of Lebanon's Amal militia, Nabih Berri

more than 1,500 prisoners. The hijacking was over, and Hezbollah had achieved its goals—worldwide publicity and the freeing of Shi'ite and Palestinian prisoners from Israeli jails.

Another Hezbollah action was the taking of single hostages. Hezbollah used these hostages for publicity and diplomacy by kidnapping western Europeans and U.S. citizens who were living and working in Beirut.

On March 16, 1984, Hezbollah seized William Buckley, the chief of the CIA bureau in Beirut. Instead of demanding ransom, the kidnappers put Buckley on trial and executed him. (This may have been an act of revenge for the CIA's attack on Sheikh Fadlallah, which had occurred only a few days before.) Over the next few years, Hezbollah took more than a dozen British, French, and American hostages. The group held most of them captive for many years.

In September 1985, Hezbollah also began targeting citizens of the Soviet Union, a close ally of Syria. The organization kidnapped four Soviet officials working in Lebanon and killed one of them. By doing this, Hezbollah hoped to pressure the Soviet Union into stopping Syria's attacks in Lebanon.

The Soviets reacted quickly. After evacuating all their personnel from the country, they arranged the kidnapping and murder of one of Sheikh Fadlallah's relatives. A few days later, Hezbollah released its hostages. The group never again targeted Soviet citizens in Lebanon.

Although Hezbollah was growing, its activities were drawing attention from police agencies in Europe. On September 13, 1987, the German police arrested Mohammad Hammadi, a member of Hezbollah. At the time he wes carrying several bottles of liquid explosives. While holding Hammadi, the police identified him as one of the hijackers of TWA Flight 847. Hammadi's fingerprints had been found on the plane, and a TWA hostage had positively identified him.

Shortly after the arrest, Hezbollah kidnapped two West German citizens in Lebanon. The group then demanded Hammadi's release, and the West German government gave in to the terrorists by allowing the

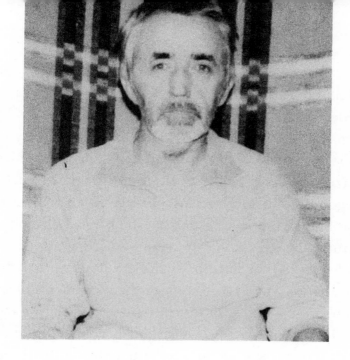

Hezbollah released this photograph of Beirut CIA chief William Buckley, whom they kidnapped and later killed.

employer of one of their hostages to pay a $2 million ransom.

Acting as an agent of Iran, Hezbollah also targeted French citizens in Lebanon. A series of 1985 bombings in Paris had terrified its citizens. After the bombings, the French police identified an Iranian, Wahid Gordji, as one of the men responsible for the bomb attacks. When the French demanded his prompt surrender from the Iranian embassy in Paris, Iran responded by surrounding the French embassy in Teheran, the Iranian capital.

The governments of France and Iran were at a

standoff. Although embassies were traditionally private property, the Revolutionary Guards had seized the U.S. embassy in Teheran in 1979 and taken the embassy staff hostage for more than a year. Seeking to avoid the seizure of their embassy, France's leaders decided to negotiate with the Iranians. France asked Iran to free the French captives held by Hezbollah in Lebanon. In return, the French government allowed Wahid Gordji to leave the Iranian embassy in Paris and return to Iran. In addition, the French stopped their shipments of arms to Iraq, a country with which Iran was fighting a war.

Despite its successes, Hezbollah began to lose support among Shi'ites in southern Lebanon in the late 1980s. The clerics who led Hezbollah refused to make any alliances with other Muslim factions in Lebanon. Hezbollah found that, with fewer recruits and with many of its fighters still being held in foreign prisons, it could no longer operate outside of Lebanon.

In the autumn of 1986, Hezbollah made its greatest mistake. The group kidnapped and tortured a large group of Syrian fighters in Beirut. After the organization released the soldiers, Syria formed an alliance with Amal to rid the capital of Hezbollah fighters. In February 1987, Syria's army invaded a Hezbollah-controlled neighborhood and massacred dozens of guerrillas. A year later, Hezbollah fought a long battle with Amal and the Syrians for control of southern Beirut. After several days of savage street-to-street fighting, Hezbollah was forced to abandon the city.

At the same time, the Iranian government was losing its enthusiasm for Hezbollah. After Khomeini died in June 1989, the new Iranian president, Hashemi Rafsanjani, changed his country's stance toward the Western nations. Rafsanjani needed to rebuild his country after the long war with Iraq. For this, trade with the West was essential. Iran convinced Hezbollah's kidnappers to free their British, French, German, and American hostages. Terry Anderson, the last hostage, was released on December 4, 1991.

As the Lebanese civil war came to an end in the late 1980s, an agreement between the Lebanese government, the Syrian government, and many of Lebanon's private militias ended the open warfare. With the civil war at an end and the Iranian government pressuring the group for the release of its hostages, Hezbollah gradually lost its influence.

Although Hezbollah has survived in south Lebanon, the movement now has only a few hundred guerrillas. And while its terrorist acts are fewer, Hezbollah has thrived as a political organization. Several Hezbollah leaders won election to Lebanon's parliament in 1992, after a cease-fire came into effect. To acheive their goals, Sheikh Fadlallah and Hezbollah now also find themselves fighting in the less deadly field of politics.

Once a professor, Abimael Guzman of Peru's Shining Path terrorist group poses for this police mug shot.

9

Abimael Guzman
and the Shining Path

*T*he city of Lima is a sprawling capital of six million people that lies near the coast of the Pacific Ocean. The capital of the South American nation of Peru, Lima attracts thousands of new residents each day. Most of these new arrivals are poor people from the countryside. They live in shantytowns and build their homes out of cardboard and thin sheets of metal. They have no bathrooms, electricity, or running water. Many make their living as thieves or beggars on Lima's downtown streets.

Residents of Lima, whether they are rich or poor, have seen many strange and terrible events. But on a December day in 1980, they woke to an unforgettable sight. As the sun came up, dozens of dogs were found hanging from the city's streetlamps. The dogs were strays that had been shot or strangled. Small cardboard signs carrying political slogans about the communist leaders of China were hanging around their necks. Also written on the signs was the name of a shadowy underground group—*Sendero Luminoso*, or the Shining Path.

Sendero Luminoso was born in Ayacucho, a department (state) of Peru that lies high in the Andes Mountains. Ayacucho is an isolated place with a large population of Peruvian Indians, who are descended from the ancient Incas. Ever since the conquest of the Incas by the Spanish in the sixteenth century, Ayacucho has been the site of many Indian rebellions. During the twentieth century, Ayacucho and other remote areas of Peru also became the scene of warfare between the Peruvian government and guerrillas fighting in the name of communism.

Shining Path was not the creation of Indians, nor was its founder—Abimael Guzman—a guerrilla. Guzman was born in 1934, in the department of Arequipa. He attended a Roman Catholic high school and San Augustin University in the city of Arequipa. There he studied law and philosophy and earned degrees in both subjects.

In the 1950s, Guzman and many other university students in Latin America found inspiration in the communist revolutions of the Soviet Union and China. In 1959, a Communist fighter named Fidel Castro led a small but dedicated band of followers into the city of

Cuba's Fidel Castro (seated) influenced many revolutionary movements in Latin America. By the 1990s, his brutal dictatorship had brought extreme misery to the Cuban people.

Havana to overthrow the government of Cuba. Castro became a hero to many people in Latin America, including Abimael Guzman. Fired by Castro's example, Guzman joined the Communist party of Peru, an organization founded by Jose Carlos Mariategui.

Guzman was a brilliant and hardworking student. His future, his teachers believed, lay in the academic world. In 1962, he became an assistant professor at the National University of San Cristóbal de Huamanga in Ayacucho. Although he was a philosophy professor, his classes discussed only politics. He described his dream

143

of remaking Peru in the image of China—a society in which there were no rich and poor fighting for money and jobs, and where the communists were said to have ended poverty and crime. Guzman saved his highest praise for Mao Tse-tung, the ruler of Communist China.

During the next few years, Guzman gained a large and loyal following of students and fellow professors. As a reward, he was promoted to director of personnel. In this job, he managed gradually to take over the university. He hired only those professors who agreed with his political beliefs and used his position to recruit new members to his group. He fired all those who disagreed with him or who became his rivals for power within the Communist party or the university.

At the same time, China and the Soviet Union were becoming rival powers. The Soviet leaders had made changes in their society—changes that Mao harshly criticized. In 1964, Guzman left the Communist party to join *Bandera Rosa* (Red Flag), a group loyal to Mao's ideas. In the 1960s, this "Maoist" party sent Guzman to China, where he learned how to make a communist revolution in the countryside.

After returning to Peru, Guzman began criticizing Bandera Rosa's leaders, who favored a revolution in the cities among factory workers and the urban poor. Instead, Guzman saw Peru's future revolution taking place in the countryside, where most of Peru's peasants and Indians lived.

In 1970, the leaders of Bandera Rosa expelled Guzman from the group. Guzman struck out on his own, calling his new organization the "Communist Party of Peru for the Shining Path of Jose Carlos Mariategui." Guzman and his followers—Sendero Luminoso—claimed to be following the "path" intended by the founder of Peru's Communist party.

In the 1970s, Guzman began recruiting the Indians of Ayacucho to his group. Sendero members founded new cells of the organization in nearby departments as well as in Lima. The group carried out much of its recruiting in Peru's universities. Professors loyal to the Shining Path organized the students into study groups and carefully explained Guzman's ideas and plans. Many who agreed to join the Shining Path became messengers. Others became spies in regular businesses or in government agencies. New recruits also had to pass a final test—the murder of a policeman.

By 1980, Guzman was preparing to strike at the Peruvian government. Posters and graffiti calling for an armed revolution appeared on the walls of Ayacucho. Shining Path's first operation took place on May 17, 1980, during the presidential elections. Guzman arranged the bombing of polling places in Chuschi, a village in the high Andes. The group also carried out attacks on government offices, power stations, and electrical transmission lines.

At first, Guzman and the Shining Path gained little notice from the government or the people of Lima.

Sendero never took credit for its actions and remained underground and secretive. This secrecy allowed the movement to grow quickly. In remote regions where the government was weak, Sendero took over town halls, businesses, and farms.

Guzman had total control over Sendero's strategy and planned most of its operations. He based his program on the methods of Chairman Mao, the Chinese leader. After Guzman's revolution, Sendero would establish a new economy in which money would no longer exist and all transactions would be made in barter (an exchange of goods). The Shining Path also planned to abolish Peru's industry, banks, and foreign trade.

The teachings of Mao Tse-tung guided Abimael Guzman in his attempt to overthrow the Peruvian government, although he would never attain the vast following that the Chinese leader had enjoyed.

During the 1980s, the organization gradually grew stronger. In rural areas, Sendero guerrillas used torture, kidnapping, and murder to carry out Guzman's plan. They shot landowners and turned private land over to peasants in small parcels. All trade with other regions came to a halt, and the guerrillas forced farmers to plant only enough for their own families and for their villages. In this way, areas under Sendero's control became completely isolated from other regions of the country.

The central government finally took action in the Ayacucho region, where Sendero's bombings were throwing the city into chaos. In October 1981, the government declared a state of emergency in Ayacucho. The police enforced a curfew and arrested people without charging them or bringing them to trial. More than 1,000 soldiers of the Peruvian Civil Guard arrived in Ayacucho to impose order. The army of Peru responded to the Sendero threat with a terror campaign of its own—arresting, torturing, and murdering many civilians suspected of helping the Shining Path.

As the violence worsened, the prisons of Peru became centers of recruiting for Guzman. In March 1982, Sendero staged a raid on a Lima prison. The battle between the guerrillas and the prison guards lasted five hours. While many prisoners were killed, more than 200 escaped. Afterwards, Sendero began to step up its attacks on other cities and in the capital. The group bombed police stations, army barracks, and the palace of the Peruvian president. In August 1982, Sendero blew

Near their hideouts in the Peruvian Andes, members of the Shining Path pose for the camera. Taken in 1984, this is the first known photograph of the group.

up transmission towers that carried electricity along the coast of Peru. For two days, half of the country's population had no electricity.

In Lima, teams of Shining Path guerrillas drove down the streets, hurling bombs into shops, banks, and public buildings. In another attack in December, four electric towers near the city were destroyed, and the lights of the capital fell dark. On a hill rising above the city, the communist symbol of a hammer and sickle, illuminated by hundreds of torches, burnt brightly. Without light, the residents of Lima could clearly see the symbol that Sendero guerrillas had lit to celebrate Abimael Guzman's 48th birthday.

The Shining Path had brought its campaign of terror to the capital. Movie theaters, restaurants, and shops were bombed. Sendero guerrillas gunned down police and civilians in the streets. In the countryside, Sendero targeted remote cities, moving its arms and men into a single region to create a "zone of liberation." It kidnapped and quickly executed government officials. On lampposts and on the walls of shops and homes, the guerrillas posted "death notices," listing all those whom they plannned to round up and bring to trial. Anyone finding his or her name on one of these posters fled the country as quickly as possible.

To pay for its arms and explosives, Sendero guerrillas staged bank robberies and forced rural villagers to make "donations" to their cause. Villages that refused to submit to Shining Path's demands suffered the consequences. One such place was Lucanamarca, a small village in the Andes Mountains. In April 1983, after the peasants of Lucanamarca refused to support his organization, Guzman ordered several dozen guerrillas into the village. Seventy people took refuge in a church in the village's main square. Shining Path soldiers entered the church and used axes and knives to murder everyone in it. The massacre of Lucanamarca was intended as an example to other peasants in the region. Anyone who resisted the Shining Path risked death.

Many villages that joined the Shining Path did so out of desperation. The economy of the country was a shambles, and the central government seemed to care little about regions outside of Lima. Schools fell into disrepair. Roads were impassable, and even water and electricity were scarce. Many peasants barely survived on meager incomes or charity.

In the late 1980s, the government of Peru responded to the threat by sending army divisions into regions where the Shining Path was active. But the government was not able to field enough troops to wipe out the rebellion. Instead, the police raids and the imprisonment of many innocent people turned rural Peruvians against the government and into the ranks of the Shining Path.

Yet Guzman's own policies worked against the Shining Path. The leader refused to associate with any other guerrilla groups in either Peru or in neighboring countries. He gained no support from the communist nations of North Korea, China, or Cuba. His organization had to steal or force from villagers in the "liberated zone" the arms and money that it needed.

Guzman also refused to join any of the country's many opposition parties. All those who associated with him had to give their complete obedience to the Shining Path. Guzman would not share power with anyone and did not prepare anyone to carry on his programs. His devoted followers were prepared only to follow him to victory—or to death.

Shining Path eventually succeeded in creating a "liberated zone" that stretched all along the Andes Mountains, from north to south through the middle of the country. From this region, Guzman planned to undertake a campaign of terror that would cause an uprising in the countryside. From their strongholds in the mountains and valleys, Shining Path guerrillas would have surrounded and besieged the cities of the coast and the capital. A network of urban terrorists would bomb the cities, causing anarchy and, eventually, the fall of the government.

Gradually, the people of Peru began to despair of ever freeing themselves from Guzman's bloody revolution. The movement was attracting students, peasants, professors, labor leaders, and even lawyers and doctors. By the summer of 1992, Shining Path was planning a campaign of terror in the capital. In July and August, bombs exploded in Lima's streets, stores, and police stations. People were terrorized, and transportation systems were forced to close down.

The Shining Path seemed to be nearing its goal of completely disrupting the country. But the campaign also brought Abimael Guzman down into Lima from his hideout in the Andes Mountains. Helped by informants and by Shining Path guerrillas in captivity, the police began a massive search for him.

By mid-September, they had discovered a Shining Path headquarters in a middle-class Lima neighborhood. To watch the house, police agents dressed in plain clothes and posed as street-sweepers, residents, and passersby. One evening, a policeman spotted what he believed was Guzman's profile in a window of the house. A few days later, a group of Guzman's friends were spotted knocking on the front door.

151

The police were ready. Several drew their guns and rushed into the house. In an upstairs room, they found Guzman, unarmed and unprepared. The police also found several of his aides and his second-in-command. The founder and leader of the Shining Path meekly surrendered to the captain of the police, who promptly rushed his captive to a Lima prison.

For several weeks, the government placed Guzman on display. His photograph appeared in many newspapers and on television. Peru's leaders, including President Alberto Fujimori, intended to show Guzman to the members of the Shining Path and to the people of Peru as an overweight, middle-aged, and powerless man. Instead of leading a revolution, Guzman was now standing behind bars in a prison cell, shouting helplessly at his guards. In October 1992, Peru's highest court sentenced him to spend the rest of his life at El Fronton, a prison island off the coast near the capital.

Although the Shining Path lost its founder, the organization has endured. Its goals have not changed—the new Shining Path leaders still work to disrupt Peruvian society and to destroy the country's government.

In January 1993, Shining Path marked a series of local elections with a day of murderous bombings and carefully planned assassinations. Targets included the Peruvian headquarters of IBM in Lima, where a car bomb explosion injured 15 people. Abimael Guzman's ideas and methods have survived his capture, and the people of Peru still fear the Shining Path.

His terrorist career apparently over, Abimael Guzman rants and raves in a Peruvian jail.

Bibliography

Becker, Jillian. *Hitler's Children: The Story of the Baader-Meinhof Terrorist Gang.* New York: Lippincott, 1977.

Forester, Margery. *Michael Collins: The Lost Leader.* London: Sidgwick and Jackson, 1971.

Katz, Robert. *Days of Wrath: The Ordeal of Aldo Moro.* Garden City, NY: Doubleday, 1980.

Laqueur, Walter and Alexander, Yonah. *The Terrorism Reader.* New York: NAL Penguin, 1987.

Long, David E. *The Anatomy of Terrorism.* New York: The Free Press, 1990.

Melman, Yosi. *The Master Terrorist: The True Story Behind Abu Nidal.* New York: Adama Books, 1986.

O'Connor, Frank. *The Big Fellow: Michael Collins and the Irish Revolution.* Dublin: Clonmore and Reynolds, 1965.

Pomper, Philip. *Sergei Nechaev.* New Brunswick, NJ: Rutgers University Press, 1979.

Raynor, Thomas. *Terrorism: Past, Present, Future.* New York: Franklin Watts, 1987.

Seale, Patrick. *Abu Nidal: A Gun for Hire.* New York: Random House, 1992.

Smith, Colin. *Carlos: Portrait of a Terrorist.* New York: Holt, Rinehart, and Winston, 1977.

Sterling, Claire. *The Terror Network: The Secret War of International Terrorism.* New York: Holt, Rinehart, and Winston, 1981.

Stefoff, Rebecca. *Yasir Arafat.* New York: Chelsea House, 1988.

Wallach, Janet and John. *Arafat: In the Eyes of the Beholder.* New York: Lyle Stuart, 1990.

Index

Abu Dawud, 83, 84
Abu Nidal (Sabri Khalil al-
Banna): as agent of Iraq, 82,
87; as agent of Libya, 91, 92,
93; as agent of Syria, 88-90;
attacks of, against Jordan, 89-
90; early years of, 77-78; and
massacre at Rome airport,
74, 76, 77; as member of
Fatah, 79-80; as member of
PLO, 80-82; opposition of,
to Arafat, 80, 81-82, 84, 85;
and seizure of Saudi embassy,
83-84
Act of Union, 29
Arafat, Yasir: as diplomat, 44,
51-53, 54, 57, 85, 88; early
years of, 44-45; in Egypt, 45-
46; as leader of Fatah, 47-49,
52, 78-79, 82; as leader of the
PLO, 42, 47, 49, 50-51, 53,
54, 55, 57, 61, 80, 81, 84, 91;
terrorist activities of, 45, 50,
51-52
Alexander II (tsar of Russia), 9,
22, 23; assassination of, 22-
25
Algeria, 63, 71, 72, 73, 133, 134
Allush, Naji, 86-87
Amal, 127, 128, 133, 138
Amerio, Ettore, 114
Anderson, Terry, 139
Andreotti, Giulio, 119-120
Arabs, 43, 44, 47, 48; in
Palestine, 43, 44, 45, 47, 79
el-Assad, Hafez, 88, 90
Austria, terrorists activities in,
64, 65, 70, 71-72, 76
Ayacucho, Peru, 142, 145, 147

Baader, Bernd Andreas, 97, 98,
99, 100, 101, 102; death of,
107; imprisonment of, 97, 99,
100, 105, 106; as member of

Baader-Meinhof Gang, 101,
102, 103
Baader-Meinhof Gang, 102,
107; bank robberies of, 102-
103; formation of, 101; ter-
rorist attacks of, 103-104.
See also Red Army Faction.
Ba'ath party, 78, 82, 86
Bakunin, Mikhail, 17-18, 21
Bandera Rosa, 144-145
al-Banna, Khalil, 77
al-Banna, Sabri Khalil, 77-79.
See also Abu Nidal.
Beirut, 42, 54, 88, 128, 131,
134, 135, 138; attack on U.S.
Marine barracks at, 125, 131
Berlin, 96, 100, 101; student
demonstrations in 96-97
Berlinguer, Enrico, 111-112
Berri, Nabih, 134, 135
Black-and-Tans, 35
Black September, 51, 52, 64
Bloody Sunday, 37
Boudia, Mohammad, 63-64
brigatistas, 114, 115, 120, 123
Broy, Ned, 35
Bseiso, Atef, 93
Buckley, William, 135, 137

Cagol, Margherita, 113, 116,
117
Carlos. *See* Ramirez Sanchez,
Ilich.
Castro, Fidel, 142-143
Catechism of a Revolutionary, 18-
19
Catholics, Irish, 29, 30, 38, 40
China, 142, 144, 146
Christian Democratic party
(Italy), 111, 112, 116, 120
CIA, 131, 135
Collins, Michael: assassination
of, 27, 28, 37; early years of,
27, 30; and Easter Rebellion,

102, 127-128
Reign of Terror, 9, 10
Rejection Front, 61, 62
republicans, Irish, 29-34, 37
revolution, 7, 13; in 1848, 13-
  14; French, 7, 8, 13, 29, 95;
  in Russia, 14, 15, 17, 25; violence used in, 7-8, 17, 59, 97,
  99, 111
Revolutionary Guards, 126,
  127, 138
Robespierre, Maximilien, 7, 8,
  13
Rome airport, massacre at, 74,
  75-76, 91
Russia, 9, 13; revolutionary
  activities in, 14, 15, 16, 19,
  23-24

Saddam Hussein, 55, 56,87
"safe house," 39, 65, 66
St. Petersburg, 15, 16, 21, 22,
  23
Saudi Arabia, 57, 70, 72, 78, 79,
  83
Schleyer, Hans Martin, 106,
  107
Schonau transit camp, 64, 65
Sendero Luminoso. *See*
  Shining Path
Shi'ite Muslims, 126, 127-128,
  130, 133, 138
Shining Path, 140, 142, 146,
  151, 152, 153; founding of,
  145; terrorist activities of,
  145; 147-149, 150
Sinn Féin, 33, 34, 40
Six-Day War (1967), 44, 48, 49,
  53, 61, 88
Society of the People's
  Revenge, 19, 20
Sossi, Mario, 114-115
Soviet Union, 60, 73, 95, 97,
  112, 136, 142, 144

Spain, 109
Stammheim Prison, 105
Stetham, Robert, 134
Sudan, 80
Syria, 44, 47, 48, 54, 84, 86, 88,
  89, 90; involvement of, in
  Lebanon, 127, 129, 134, 136,
  138-139

Tel Aviv airport, massacre at,
  66, 67
television, use of, by terrorists,
  9, 51, 133, 134
Thatcher, Margaret, 38
Third Section, 16, 21, 23
Torrejon, Spain, terrorist attack
  in, 132
truck bomb, 125, 130, 131
tsar, Russian, 13, 14, 15, 18, 22,
  23, 24, 25
TWA Flight 847, hijacking of,
  133-135, 136

Ulster, 28, 37, 38, 40
United Arab Emirates (UAE),
  86, 87, 90
United Irishmen, 29
United Kingdom, 29, 30, 34, 37
United Nations, 53, 85
United States, 56, 112, 120,
  125, 129, 131, 132
Vienna airport, terrorist attack
  at, 76, 91
Vietnam War, 96, 99

West Bank, 48, 49, 54, 55, 56,
  61, 77, 79
World War I, 30-31, 34, 43
World War II, 9, 95, 111

Yom Kippur War (1973), 52

Zayid, Sheikh, 90

Photo Credits

ABOUT THE AUTHOR

TOM STREISSGUTH, born in Washington, D.C., in 1958, attended Yale University as a student of history, literature, languages, and music. He has traveled widely in Europe and the Middle East, and has worked as a teacher, editor, and journalist. His most recent book, *Soviet Leaders from Lenin to Gorbachev*, was published in 1992 by The Oliver Press.